What Is
Narrative Criticism?

What
Is
Narrative
Criticism?

by
Mark Allan Powell

Fortress Press
Minneapolis

WHAT IS NARRATIVE CRITICISM?

Copyright © 1990 Augsburg Fortress. All rights reserved. Except for brief quotations
in critical articles or reviews, no part of this book may be reproduced in any manner
without prior written permission from the publisher. Write to: Permissions, Augsburg
Fortress, 426 S. Fifth St., Box 1209, Minneapolis, MN 55440.

Scripture quotations unless otherwise noted are from the Revised Standard Version of
the Bible, copyright © 1946, 1952, and 1971 by the Division of Chrisitian Education of
the National Council of Churches.

Library of Congress Cataloging-in-Publication Data

Powell, Mark Allan, 1953–
    What is narrative criticism? / by Mark Allan Powell.
        p.   cm.—(Guides to biblical scholarship)
    Includes bibliographical references and index.
    ISBN 0-8006-0473-3 (alk. paper) : $7.95
    1. Bible—Criticism, Narrative.   I. Title.   II. Series.
BS521.7.P68   1990
220.6'6—dc20
                                                                90-13863
                                                                CIP

The paper used in this publication meets the minimum requirements of American
National Standard for Information Sciences—Permanence of Paper for Printed Library
Materials, ANSI Z329.48–1984.   ∞™

Manufactured in the U.S.A.   AF 1-473

94   93   92   91   90   1   2   3   4   5   6   7   8   9   10

For Charlotte

Contents

Editor's Foreword

This volume on narrative criticism continues the program of this series, which has been to *focus* on issues that are relatively broad and formal rather than on one or a few specific texts. That has not meant that practical interpretation has not been used to exemplify the categories under discussion, and so in this volume also the interpretive applications of the critical principles to particular texts are often both relatively lengthy and very illuminating. The previous volumes in the series to which this one bears the closest relationships are Beardslee, *Literary Criticism of the New Testament;* Petersen, *Literary Criticism for New Testament Critics;* and Patte, *Structural Exegesis for New Testament Critics.*

Professor Powell helpfully clarifies the distinction between literary criticism and several modes (source, form, and redaction) of historical criticism and also distinguishes several types of literary criticism (structuralist, rhetorical, reader-response, and narrative). He then goes on to describe, analyze, and illustrate the categories that narrative criticism employs—implied author and reader, narrator, characters, events, settings, and so forth.

DAN O. VIA
Duke Divinity School

Acknowledgments

In recent years, I have had numerous occasions to discuss the topic of this book in churches and in classrooms. I wish now to express my appreciation to the students of Trinity Lutheran Seminary and to the pastors and laypersons throughout central Ohio who listened to my views as they were being developed.

I am grateful to Dan O. Via for supporting me in this project and for providing me with needed editorial assistance. In addition, David Bauer, Barbara Jurgensen, Jack Kingsbury, and David Rhoads took time to read my manuscript, in whole or in part, and to make helpful suggestions for its improvement. I also wish to thank Timothy Staveteig and others at Fortress Press who have guided the project through to its completion. Before his untimely death in 1989, John Hollar had occasion to read the entire manuscript and to offer valuable encouragement and advice.

Melissa Curtis, manager of computer services and secretary to the faculty at Trinity Lutheran Seminary, has done most of the work of preparing the manuscript. I continue to be grateful not only for the competence but also for the encouraging optimism and dedication that she brings to every task.

1

Scripture
as Story

A scribe who has been trained for the kingdom of heaven, Jesus once said, is like a householder who brings out of his treasure what is new and what is old. The last few years of biblical scholarship have witnessed many such scribes producing many such treasures: some are new, some are old, and some, perhaps, are both at the same time. Narrative criticism is a new approach to the Bible, but it is based on ideas that have been used in the study of other literature for some time.[1]

THE BIBLE AND LITERARY CRITICISM

In a sense, the Bible has always been studied as literature because, after all, that is what it is—scriptures or writings. The field of biblical criticism knows no methodology that circumvents the act of reading or hearing the text. Nevertheless, the Bible's literary qualities themselves have not been a typical subject for investigation. Rather, the Bible has been read as a record of significant history, a compendium of revealed truth, or a guidebook for daily living. The considerations that caused its various books to become regarded as canonical in the first place were no doubt diverse, but there is no evidence that aesthetic appreciation was among them. Indeed, St. Augustine bemoaned the low literary quality that the biblical writings evince when they are compared to the pagan works of Greece and Rome, a circumstance that he could accept only as indicative of divine humility (*Confessions* 3.5).

The discovery of literary criticism by biblical scholars, then, is something of an innovation, for it involves a self-conscious reading of the Bible in a way that it has not usually been read. The reasons for

1

this sudden convergence of biblical and literary studies must be understood in terms of recent developments in both fields.[2]

The dominant mode of biblical studies for more than a century has been the historical-critical method.[3] Actually a conglomeration of approaches, this method seeks to reconstruct the life and thought of biblical times through an objective, scientific analysis of biblical material. Source criticism, for example, attempts to delineate the sources that the evangelists used in the composition of their Gospels. Form criticism concentrates on defining the *Sitz im Leben* (setting in life) that individual units of tradition may have had before they came to be incorporated into the Gospels. Redaction criticism seeks to discern the theologies and intentions of the evangelists themselves by observing the manner in which they edited their sources and arranged the individual units of tradition. These disciplines share a common desire to shed light upon significant periods in the transmission of the Gospels: the period of the historical Jesus, the period of oral tradition in the life of the early church, or the period of the final shaping of the Gospels by the evangelists.

The major limitation of all these approaches, as documented by Hans Frei in 1974, is that they fail to take seriously the narrative character of the Gospels.[4] These books are stories about Jesus, not compilations of miscellaneous data concerning him. They are intended to be read from beginning to end, not dissected and examined to determine the relative value of individual passages. In focusing on the documentary status of these books, the historical-critical method attempted to interpret not the stories themselves but the historical circumstances behind them.

The need for a more literary approach to the Gospels had been sounded in 1969 by William A. Beardslee.[5] Decrying the sharply historical cast of most biblical scholarship, Beardslee suggested that analysis of biblical forms should provide insight not only into the character of the communities that shaped these texts but also into the literary meaning and impact of the texts themselves. Form criticism should include attention to how particular literary forms work, that is, how they invite the reader to participate in the passage under consideration and attempt to evoke a particular response from that reader. The first literary forms in the New Testament to be examined in this way were the parables; some of the most important studies were those of Robert W. Funk, Dan O. Via, and John D. Crossan.[6]

2

Another concern voiced by Beardslee was the need for greater attention to the larger form of Gospel itself. The development of redaction criticism partially met this need by focusing on the role of the evangelists in assembling various traditions into coherent wholes. Whereas form criticism typically regarded the evangelists as mere collectors, redaction criticism insisted on their status as editors who were personally responsible for the finished product. As this discipline matured, appreciation for the role of the evangelists increased still further and they came to be described not only as editors but as authors. Finally, Norman Perrin was led to write, "This means we have to introduce a whole new category into our study . . . the category of general literary criticism. If the evangelists are authors, then they must be studied as other authors are studied."[7]

The desire for a more literary approach to the Gospels, then, was first expressed by historical critics themselves, in recognition of the limitations of an exclusively historical approach. The prevailing sense was not that historical criticism had failed or that its goals were invalid, but that something else should also be done. The Bible was not being studied in the same manner as other ancient literature. At most colleges and universities, for example, the works of Homer are studied by at least two different departments. Classical historians hope to extract information about the ancient world, such as how people dressed, ate, married, and went to war. But scholars of literature employ a different set of questions: What is the plot? How are characters developed? What effect does the story have on its readers and why does it have this effect? Under the dominance of historical criticism, biblical scholarship found itself limited to the concerns of a single division. New Testament professors became, in effect, an extension of the church history department. The Gospels were regarded as resources for learning about Jesus and the early church, but not as narratives that have significant stories to tell. The question, as phrased by Norman R. Petersen in 1978, was whether these texts should not first be comprehended on their own terms before they are treated as evidence of something else.[8]

Even after the need for a truly literary study of the Gospels was recognized, uncertainty persisted as to how to proceed. There are significant differences between the Gospels and the works of Homer. The problem with treating a Gospel "just like any other book"[9] is that the Gospels are not like other books. In some respects, they resemble modern novels more than modern biographies and yet it is obvious that their writers did not intend them to be viewed as fiction. To many

3

scholars, the Gospels do not appear to fit into the category of "self-consciously imaginary literature," which, according to Rene Wellek and Austin Warren's classic textbook on literary criticism, is the only type of literature subject to genuine literary analysis.[10]

This perception of the Gospels, however, had been challenged as early as 1946 by the publication of Erich Auerbach's landmark study, *Mimesis: The Representation of Reality in Western Literature*.[11] One of Auerbach's conclusions was that biblical narrative can be studied according to the canons of general literary criticism. In choosing narrative discourse as their medium, the biblical writers inevitably selected a form of expression that presents a narrative depiction of reality. This is a feature that biblical texts share with other literary works (including Homer). The representation of reality in narrative form, Auerbach proposed, is a basic element of literature that transcends traditional distinctions between aesthetic and historical purposes. What an author wishes to say about the things reported in a narrative—real or imaginary—may be discerned by observing the style of expression that is used.

The 1940s generated other developments that would prove fortuitous for biblical scholars. Prior to 1940, secular critics also paid a great deal of attention to establishing the identity, circumstances, and intentions of a work's historical author. It was considered important, for example, to know the order in which the plays of William Shakespeare or the novels of Charles Dickens were written. Any interpretation of a work by one of these masters would be expected to take into account the circumstances of its writing: the life and personality of the author at this point in his career, and perhaps the condition of English society at the time. In the 1940s, however, this manner of interpretation was by and large replaced by an approach that came to be called the New Criticism.[12]

The New Criticism rejected the notion that background information holds the interpretive key to a text. It is not necessary, for instance, to know that John Keats was caring for his dying brother when he wrote "Bright Star," a sonnet replete with themes of love and death.[13] When this knowledge is imposed upon the sonnet, in fact, it becomes a distraction, an intrusion that prevents the work from being read on its own terms. The New Critics held that the author's intention is "irrelevant to the literary critic, because meaning and value reside within the text of the finished, free-standing, and public work of literature itself."[14] Most literary critics today have moved beyond the

4

initial concerns of New Criticism and many would regard the position just stated as extreme. Even so, it is now accepted as axiomatic in literary circles that the meaning of literature transcends the historical intentions of the author.[15]

Literary critics today prefer to speak of an *implied author*, who is reconstructed by the reader from the narrative.[16] When a person reads a story, he or she will inevitably form some impression about that story's author. The story itself conveys a sense of the author's values and worldview. For example, anyone who reads John Bunyan's *Pilgrim's Progress* or Dante's *Inferno* will no doubt conclude that the authors are Christians. Impressions like these define what literary critics refer to as the implied author of a narrative. The goal of such a definition, however, is not to arrive at a partial understanding of what the real author might have been like, but to elucidate the perspective from which the narrative must be interpreted. The implied author's point of view can be determined without considering anything extrinsic to the narrative. Thus, literary critics may speak of the intentions of the implied author without violating the basic principle that narratives should be interpreted on their own terms. When hermeneutical preference is given to a work's implied author over its real, historical author, the narrative is allowed to speak for itself. The interpretive key no longer lies in background information, but within the text itself.

The development of this concept of the implied author has led to many important conclusions for the study of literature. For example, when an author produces a work that espouses values at variance with his or her actual point of view, most scholars agree that the perspective of the implied author still determines what the story means. A critic may recognize by way of historical footnote that the person who wrote this story did not actually think this way, but, nevertheless, the story means what the story means. Again, the distinction between implied authors and real authors becomes significant when more than one work by the same writer is to be considered. Even though Robert Louis Stevenson wrote both *Treasure Island* and *Dr. Jeckyl and Mr. Hyde*, the implied authors of these two novels are not identical.

Distinctions of this sort become less important in studies of the New Testament Gospels since no two of these works have the same author[17] and there is no reason to believe that the real authors did not fully accept the ideas expressed in their books. Of more significance is the premise that identification of the implied author provides all that is needed in order to comprehend the literary meaning and impact of the narrative; thus it is possible to understand works that are anonymous. All narratives have an implied author, even if the real author is unknown. Even stories that have no real author—such as tales that have developed over a period of time by being passed down from generation to generation—can be studied according to the standards of narrative criticism.[18] This is true because, regardless of the process through which a narrative comes into being, it will have a single implied author, which can be identified and described.

Secular literary critics themselves did not show great interest in studying the New Testament Gospels as literature,[19] but the consensus among them by the early 1970s seemed to be that there was no good reason why such a thing could not be done. It seemed inevitable, then, that the need for a literary approach to the Gospels felt in biblical circles and the possibility for such an approach recognized in secular circles would eventually come together. They did so, among other places, in the classroom. At Carthage College in 1977 a young Bible professor named David Rhoads invited a colleague from the English department to show his students what it would be like to read one of the Gospels the way one would read a short story. The presentation by Don Michie was eye-opening not only for the students, but for Rhoads as well. Ultimately, it led to the publication in 1982 of *Mark As Story*,[20] a collaborative effort by these two scholars that, more than any previously published work, demonstrated the possibilities of reading a Gospel in this way.[21] The next year saw the publication of Jack D. Kingsbury's *The Christology of Mark's Gospel*[22] and R. Alan Culpepper's *Anatomy of the Fourth Gospel*,[23] two works that consciously followed the approach Rhoads had decided to call "narrative criticism."[24] A few years later, Kingsbury also produced a major narrative study of Matthew and Robert C. Tannehill contributed a similar analysis of Luke-Acts.[25] Although the method is practiced by many scholars today who are making significant contributions, these four—Rhoads, Kingsbury, Culpepper, and Tannehill—deserve recognition as pioneers of the discipline; they have provided the first comprehensive treatments of the New Testament's five narrative books.[26]

LITERARY CRITICISM AND HISTORICAL CRITICISM

The relationship between modern literary approaches to the Bible and traditional historical-critical methodology is somewhat ambiguous. On the one hand, the literary approaches may be viewed as logical

6

developments within and extensions of form and redaction criticism. On the other hand, these newer literary approaches incorporate concepts derived from movements in secular literary criticism that repudiate the significance of historical investigation for the interpretation of texts.

The major differences between literary criticism[27] and historical criticism are worth noting here.

1. *Literary criticism focuses on the finished form of the text.* The objective of literary-critical analysis is not to discover the process through which a text has come into being but to study the text that now exists. In historical-critical research, the compositional history of the text is usually significant. Source criticism, by definition, is devoted to defining and evaluating the materials that preceded our current Gospels and served as sources for them. Form criticism is interested in the traditional form that a pericope assumed before being incorporated into the framework of a particular Gospel. Redaction criticism maintains both these interests in order to better assess the role of the evangelist in the text's final stage of composition. Literary criticism does not deny these observations regarding the development of the text, but it does ignore them. Ultimately, it makes no difference for a literary interpretation whether certain portions of the text once existed elsewhere in some other form. The goal of literary criticism is to interpret the current text, in its finished form.[28]

2. *Literary criticism emphasizes the unity of the text as a whole.* Literary analysis does not dissect the text but discerns the connecting threads that hold it together. The Gospels are viewed as coherent narratives and individual passages are interpreted in terms of their contribution to the story as a whole. In historical criticism, the Gospels are viewed as compilations of loosely related pericopes, and these individual units of tradition are most often the subject of analysis. In source criticism and form criticism, an attempt is made to interpret particular sayings or stories apart from their context in the Gospel as a whole. Even in redaction criticism, sometimes more attention is paid to comparisons between a passage and its parallels in the other Gospels than to the internal connections it may have to other passages in the same book.[29]

3. *Literary criticism views the text as an end in itself.* The immediate goal of a literary study is to understand the narrative. The story that is told and the manner in which it is told deserve full scholarly attention. Historical criticism inevitably treats the text as a means to

an end rather than as an end in itself. The "end" for historical criticism is a reconstruction of something to which the text attests, such as the life and teaching of Jesus, the interests of the early Christians who preserved traditions concerning him, or the concerns of the evangelists and their communities.

The difference between these approaches has been aptly described through the metaphors of a window and a mirror.[30] Historical criticism regards the text as a window through which the critic hopes to learn something about another time and place. The text, then, stands between the reader and the insight that is sought and may provide the means through which that insight can be obtained. Literary criticism, in contrast, regards the text as a mirror; the critic determines to look at the text, not through it, and whatever insight is obtained will be found in the encounter of the reader with the text itself.

Literary criticism, it is sometimes said, deals with the poetic function of a text, whereas historical criticism deals with its referential function. This means that literary critics are able to appreciate the story of a narrative apart from consideration of the extent to which it reflects reality. The story world of the narrative is to be entered and experienced rather than evaluated in terms of historicity. In the New Testament Gospels, God speaks audibly from heaven, fantastic miracles are commonplace, and human beings interact freely with spiritual creatures like angels and demons. Such features have sometimes been problematic for historical critics who evaluate the Gospel narratives in terms of their referential function, that is, their ability to refer to the real world. The literary critic, however, is interested in the contribution that these elements make to the story and in discerning the effect that such a story has on its readers.

This does not mean that literary critics question the legitimacy of historical inquiry. It should not be assumed that they naively accept whatever they read as perfectly historical or that they view the Bible as a collection of tales with little basis in reality. Rather, these critics bracket out questions of historicity in order to concentrate on the nature of the text as literature. They do not deny that biblical narratives may also serve a referential function or that it may be rewarding to study them in that regard as well.

4. *Literary criticism is based on communication models of speech-act theory.* The philosophical bases for literary criticism are derived from theories about communication. One of the simplest and yet most profound of these theories is a speech-act model proposed by Roman

Jakobson.[31] Every act of communication, Jakobson avers, involves a sender, a message, and a receiver. In literature, the sender may be identified with the author, the message with the text, and the receiver with the reader.

Author ⎯⎯⎯⎯⎯⎯► Text ⎯⎯⎯⎯⎯⎯► Reader

The exact way in which these components interact with each other is understood differently by different schools of literary criticism (see chap. 2). All theories of literature, however, understand the text as a form of communication through which a message is passed from the author to the reader.

Historical criticism, on the other hand, has approached texts on the basis of an evolutionary model.[32] The text is viewed as the final form of something that has evolved through sequential stages. The task of interpretation, therefore, involves an analytical process that seeks to identify these stages and to work backward through them in reconstructing a hypothetical pattern of the text's origins. In the case of the Gospels, New Testament scholars have typically postulated an evolutionary process of development similar to the following:

Historical Event
↓
Oral Tradition
↓
Early Written Sources
↓
Text

In this model, as in the communication model diagrammed above, the text may be identified as any one of our New Testament Gospels. In literary criticism, however, this text is viewed as the middle component in an act of communication, whereas in historical criticism it is regarded as the end product of a process of development. Apart from their common interest in the text, the two approaches do not overlap: the one may be regarded as dealing with a horizontal dimension of the text and the other as treating an intersecting vertical dimension.

9

It is likely that two such different approaches, based as they are on divergent philosophical models, will produce different types of insight. Literary criticism is more likely to describe the meaning of a text in terms of what it communicates between its author and its reader, and historical criticism is more likely to describe its meaning in terms of its origin and process of development. Still, these insights will not necessarily be contradictory and so potential exists for the two models to be used in ways that are distinctive but complementary.[33]

2

Ways of
Reading

Literary criticism is a broad field that encompasses a vast array of different methodologies. Just as biblical studies have seen the rise and fall of various approaches to interpretation, the history of literary criticism is replete with movements that favor particular theories. The student who decides to become a literary critic learns about such schools as Formalism, Realism, Imagism, Aestheticism, Decadence, Deconstruction, and so forth.[1] In this chapter, we will compare narrative criticism with other literary approaches being used in biblical studies: How are they similar and how are they different?

A system of categorization devised by M. H. Abrams helps to bring some order to the chaos of literary theories.[2] For Abrams, there are four basic types of literary criticism and all of the various schools may be understood as representing one or more of these four types.

1. *Expressive* types of criticism are author-centered and tend to evaluate a work in terms of the sincerity and adequacy with which it expresses the views and temperament of its writer.
2. *Pragmatic* types of criticism are reader-centered and view the work as something that is constructed in order to achieve a particular effect on its audience; the work is evaluated according to its success in achieving that aim.
3. *Objective* types of criticism are text-centered, viewing the literary product as a self-sufficient world in itself. The work must be analyzed according to intrinsic criteria, such as the inter-relationship of its component elements.
4. *Mimetic* types of criticism view the literary work as a reflection of the outer world or of human life and evaluate it in terms of the truth or accuracy of its representation.

The first three types of literary criticism described by Abrams correspond to the three components of the communication model diagrammed in chapter 1: author, text, and reader. The fourth type, furthermore, may be related to what we designated the evolutionary model, the philosophical basis for historical criticism. I have already suggested that communication and evolutionary models for interpretation are not mutually exclusive but describe, respectively, the horizontal and vertical dimensions of interpretation. Abrams's four types of literary criticism assume precisely such a cross section in the study of secular literature.

Abrams's model invites us to rethink our terminology. I have drawn the distinction between what biblical scholars call "historical criticism" and what they call "literary criticism." It is important to recognize, however, that this distinction is based on a narrow definition of literary criticism, one which literary critics themselves might not accept. Abrams would describe the difference as being between different types of literary criticism: what biblical scholars usually call historical-critical methods are referential (mimetic) and author-centered (expressive) modes of literary criticism. The new literary criticism that has invaded biblical studies in recent years is actually an incursion of methods that draw on other types of literary criticism, namely, text-centered (objective) and reader-centered (pragmatic) approaches.

Four such methods are currently being employed in studies of the New Testament Gospels: structuralism, rhetorical criticism, reader-response criticism, and narrative criticism.[3]

STRUCTURALISM

Developed primarily in France during the 1950s and 1960s, structuralism[4] is an objective type of criticism that attempts to analyze literature from the standpoint of modern linguistic theory. Historically, the movement has its roots in another approach, called Russian Formalism, which was exemplified in the work of Vladimir Propp. In a classic study of Russian folktales,[5] Propp demonstrated that, although the specific characters and the actions they perform vary in the tales, the functions of the characters and actions are essentially the same. After studying approximately 100 stories, Propp identified 31 functions that recur almost invariably in the same sequence. Even when some functions are absent in a story, the sequence of the ones that are present remains undisturbed.

Today, structuralists do not limit their study of underlying structures to the detection of simple linear arrangements such as those discovered by Propp. They search not only for syntagmatic (sequential) associations but also for paradigmatic ones, that is, for relationships within a text that exist at various levels of meaning apart from the sequential order of the narrative. The analogy of a musical score is sometimes employed: In order to be meaningful, such a score must be read not only from left to right, but also up and down, since individual notes often make up a single harmonic unit. One of the most common relationships to be discerned within texts is that of binary oppositions, schematic pairs (such as good and evil, life and death, rich and poor) that provide intrinsic structure. As indicated, such associations may be detected at various levels: some may be merely syntactical, some logical, and some connotative of the mythical system the work assumes. Structuralists conceive of texts as conglomerates of meaning with one layer of underlying structures superimposed upon another. Generally, the "deep structures" are the goal of research, for they may reveal conventions of belief in the text that transcend the conscious intentions of the author.

In a sense, structuralism is more a philosophy than it is a method. Structuralist approaches to law, sociology, and mathematics are all born of the same theoretical movement. As a school of literary criticism, structuralism attempts to devise a "grammar of literature." The goal is to understand how literature works; the assumption is that fixed laws determine this. Just as most speakers of a language do not have explicit knowledge of the rules that govern their speech, so most writers do not consciously choose to follow the laws of literature. Nevertheless, as a form of communication, literature does follow certain conventions that cause it to mean one thing or another. Thus, the meaning of a text is found within the deep structures of the text rather than in the intentions of the author or in the perceptions of the reader, who also may not fully understand the grammar of literature. By analyzing a text's communicative strategy, structuralists intend to become fully competent readers who may understand the work in a way that even the author did not.

Biblical scholars have used structuralism to elucidate the literary character of certain writings and their theological implications. For example, Daniel Patte uses his structural commentary on Matthew's Gospel[6] as a means of explicating Matthew's faith, that is, the system of convictions that the work holds to be self-evident. These convictions are best revealed in the oppositions that can be discerned within the work, such as the opposition between "new" and "old" in Matt. 9:16-17 or between "saying" and "doing" in 23:2-3. Such oppositions not only identify the main points of a passage, but also grant insight into the system of convictions that undergird the entire work.

Narrative criticism is like structuralism in that it is also a text-centered (objective) approach to literature. The concepts employed, however, are somewhat different and the philosophical basis less intense. Narrative critics do not necessarily regard the laws of literature as following elaborate structural principles. In general, they are more concerned with the linear progression of a narrative than with relationships that may be discerned on other levels. They are usually more interested in defining the surface meaning of the story than in discovering deep structures that undergird it. These distinctions are not absolute, however, and in practice the two approaches are somewhat eclectic.

RHETORICAL CRITICISM

Within literary circles, rhetorical criticism[7] is viewed as a pragmatic approach to literature that focuses on the means through which a work achieves a particular effect on its reader. The Roman poet and satirist Horace thought the purpose of writing was either to instruct or to delight the reader or, preferably, to do both.[8] Cicero mentioned a third function, to move or persuade.[9] Rhetorical critics have sought to discover how literature accomplishes these things and why it has these particular effects.

Aristotle formulated a theory that allows for the definition of three "species of rhetoric": judicial, which accuses or defends; deliberative, which gives advice; and epideictic, which praises or blames.[10] Determination of how such effects are accomplished includes examination of the types of arguments or proofs that are used, the manner in which the material is arranged, and the style in which it is presented. Rhetorical critics are interested, for example, not only in the point that a work wishes to make but also in the basis on which that point is established. Sometimes external evidence or documentation is cited or the trustworthy character of the writer is invoked. At other times, an appeal is made to the readers' emotions or sense of logic. Before such determinations can be made, however, it is necessary to identify the *rhetorical situation* that is being addressed. In rhetorical criticism it is important to know as much as possible about the circumstances of a work's intended audience. One critic has suggested that "a peculiar discourse comes into existence because of some specific condition or situation which invites utterance."[11] Since "the situation controls the rhetorical response," it is incumbent upon critics to examine the persons, events, objects, and relations that have called forth that response. It is this view of literature as response that makes rhetorical criticism a reader-centered approach: the text is understood from the perspective of those to whom it is directed.[12]

In New Testament scholarship, rhetorical criticism has been used mainly in studies of epistles or of portions of the Gospels and Acts that may be isolated as distinctive units (e.g., speeches).[13] Hans Dieter Betz, for example, compares Galatians to the judicial type of rhetoric that would have been used for defense in a contemporary court of law.[14] The classicist George Kennedy likens the Sermon on the Mount to deliberative rhetoric and Jesus' speech in John 13–17 to epideictic. He also examines the bases on which points are established in the Gospels (the evidence of miracles, the testimony of witnesses, the quotation of Scripture, and so on).[15]

Narrative criticism is similar to rhetorical criticism in that it also is interested in discerning the effect that a work has on its reader and in explicating why it has this effect. Narrative criticism, however, employs a concept of the reader that makes it a more text-centered approach. Basically, narrative criticism interprets the text from the perspective of an idealized *implied reader* who is presupposed by and constructed from the text itself. Thus, in narrative criticism it is less necessary to know the historical situation of the actual readers for whom the text was originally intended.

In addition, narrative criticism involves analysis of a different kind of rhetoric than that examined by classical scholars: the rhetoric of narrative rather than of persuasion. In *The Rhetoric of Fiction*, Wayne Booth seeks to develop a form of rhetorical criticism that is appropriate for the study of novels. He devises categories different from those of Aristotle. Instead of examining types of arguments, for example, Booth and his associates describe types of characters. They analyze plot development and identify such rhetorical devices as irony and empathy. In secular literary circles, this approach to narrative is recognized as a form of rhetorical criticism. In biblical studies, however, Booth's approach is more likely to be considered part of narrative criticism.

15

READER-RESPONSE CRITICISM

As its name implies, reader-response criticism[16] is a pragmatic approach to literature that emphasizes the role of the reader in determining meaning. More properly, reader-response criticism represents a compendium of approaches that define this role in various ways.

As recently as 1966, a major textbook on literary criticism described narrative literature as being distinguished by two characteristics, a story and a storyteller.[17] The third component of Jakobson's communication model was missing! Reader-response critics intend to correct such oversights by focusing on the activity of reading in the same way that previous literary critics focused on the activity of writing. After all, it is ultimately the readers of a text who must determine what it means. Reader-response critics study the dynamics of the reading process in order to discover how readers perceive literature and on what bases they produce or create a meaning for any given work.

Reader-response critics differ in their assessment of the factors that shape a reader's responses and especially on the extent to which the text itself determines those responses. The accompanying chart attempts to list and categorize a few of the most prominent theories, which will be discussed below.[18] As the chart indicates, many secular literary critics would view structuralism and narrative criticism as varieties of the reader-response movement. In biblical studies, however, the term reader-response criticism is normally used in reference only to the first two categories on the chart, which are more pragmatic (reader-centered) than the approaches described in the third category.

Reader-Response Theories

I.   Reader *over* the text
     1. (?) Deconstruction* (e.g., Derrida)
     2. Transactive Criticism (e.g., Holland)
     3. Interpretive Communities (e.g., late Fish)

II. Reader *with* the text
     1. Affective Stylistics (e.g., early Fish)
     2. Phenomenological Criticism (e.g., Iser)

III. Reader *in* the text
     1. Structuralism*
     2. Narrative Criticism*

*In biblical studies, these are usually regarded as independent methodologies parallel to reader-response rather than as varieties of the latter.

16

Some reader-response critics have emphasized the reader's dominance *over* the text. Since meaning is largely subjective, readers are not ultimately constrained by literary dynamics or authorial intention in their interpretation of a work. The movement known as *deconstruction* lends support to this idea. This approach is favored by scholars who became skeptical as to whether the sort of linguistic-based analysis of texts offered by structuralism could ever reveal a work's true meaning. Under the influence of Jacques Derrida,[19] they discovered that ultimately texts "deconstruct" themselves into endless labyrinths of possible meaning. Deconstruction, then, invites readers to approach texts creatively and to appreciate their ability to generate an unlimited plurality of meaningful effects. In fact, since deconstruction eventually denies that meaning can be determined even by the experience of readers, it may not belong on a chart of reader-response theories at all. Ultimately this movement "stands outside the pattern of other theories" and must be treated separately.[20]

Other reader-response critics attempt to describe the process of reading in terms of psychoanalytic concepts. Norman Holland has devised a system he calls *transactive criticism,* which understands interpretation as being largely determined by the defenses, expectations, and wish-fulfilling fantasies of the reader.[21] Thus, Holland stresses the effect of personality on perception: a reader makes sense out of a text by transforming the content in accord with his or her own identity. The text has no universal or correct meaning.

Some scholars fear that such extreme attention to the role of the reader in determining meaning will result in hermeneutical anarchy. Someone may think it is humorous, not tragic, when the two young lovers kill themselves in the final act of *Romeo and Juliet.* Someone else may think that Jesus gets what he deserves when he is crucified in the Gospel of Mark. Are there no criteria by which such interpretations may be judged misreadings? Is there no basis on which a critic can say, "That's not what the story means"? Stanley Fish has suggested one such basis in his theory of *interpretive communities.*[22] Although any single reading of a given text, is never the "right" one, agreement in interpretation does occur among those who share the same reading strategy. Within an interpretive community, then, readings may be recognized as being in or out of accord with the accepted strategy.

Reader-response criticism also includes approaches that view the role of the reader as more limited. The relationship of reader and text is dialectical, so meaning should not be viewed as something a reader

17

creates out of a text but rather as the dynamic product of the reader's interaction *with* the text. Each element (text and reader) may potentially influence and transform the other. In his early work, Fish developed a model called *affective stylistics* that described such a process of interaction.[23] He attempted to delineate what happens when a reader encounters a text in its sequential order. At any given point in the reading process, the reader will have formed conclusions about what has been read so far and will have anticipations regarding what is to come. As the reading continues, some of these anticipations will be fulfilled, while others will not. The unfulfilled anticipations represent mistaken expectations that cause the reader to revise previously held conclusions. Thus, through interaction with the text, the reader is encouraged to continually check his or her responses and revise them according to ongoing developments within the text.

A similar model developed to describe the interaction of text and reader is the *phenomenological criticism* of Wolfgang Iser.[24] Like Fish, Iser views the experience of reading as an evolving process of anticipation, frustration, retrospection, and reconstruction. Whereas Fish focused on sequential line by line reading, however, Iser is more interested in the unfolding of the work as a whole. The reader's responses are restricted by the desire to find consistency. Thus, the work contains inherent constraints against interpretations that cannot be maintained for the work as a whole as well as incentives for interpretations that can. Iser stresses, however, that these limits are only partial. The creative role of the reader is also recognized since texts contain numerous "gaps," or indeterminate elements that the reader must fill in subjectively.

Despite similarities, structuralism and narrative criticism differ from the reader-response approaches in that the former focus on ways in which the text determines the reader's response rather than on ways in which the reader determines meaning. They are therefore said to view the reader as being *in the text*, that is, encoded within it (structuralism) or presupposed by it (narrative criticism). Structuralism seeks to decipher the text's inherent codes in order to discover the response of the reader that they suggest. Narrative criticism offers another model, based on its own categories for understanding the codes and signals of the text.

18

NARRATIVE CRITICISM

Secular literary scholarship knows no such movement as *narrative criticism*. Unlike the other three approaches just discussed, this movement developed within the field of biblical studies without an exact counterpart in the secular world. If classified by secular critics, it might be viewed as a subspecies of the new rhetorical criticism or as a variety of the reader-response movement. Biblical scholars, however, tend to think of narrative criticism as an independent, parallel movement in its own right.

One of the most pressing issues in literary criticism concerns the question, Who is the reader?[25] Rhetorical criticism is interested in the original readers to whom a work was first addressed (sometimes called the *intended readers*). Structuralism wants to define the responses of a *competent reader* who understands a work's codes. Fish and Iser describe the responses of a *first-time reader* who encounters the text in its sequential order. In his later work, Fish suggests we think of *reading communities*. Many of the divergent perspectives in literary criticism today can be traced to different conceptions of the reader. When a literary critic uses the term *reader*, it is important to ask, Which reader do you mean?

Narrative critics generally speak of an *implied reader* who is presupposed by the narrative itself.[26] This implied reader is distinct from any real, historical reader in the same way that the implied author is distinct from the real, historical author. The actual responses of real readers are unpredictable, but there may be clues within the narrative that indicate an anticipated response from the implied reader. The communications model for narrative criticism, then, may be filled out as follows:

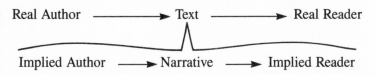

Real Author ⟶ Text ⟶ Real Reader

Implied Author ⟶ Narrative ⟶ Implied Reader

The real author and the real reader are diagrammed as lying outside the parameters of the text itself. The three middle components (Implied Author—Narrative—Implied Reader) now take the place of what was previously described simply as the text. Thus, we see that the text can be viewed either as the message component of a larger communication

19

model or as an entire communication that contains all three components (sender, message, and receiver) and so is complete in itself. Narrative criticism tends to focus on the latter understanding and thus regards the real author and the real reader as extrinsic to the communication act that transpires within the text itself. This concept of the implied reader, the reader in the text, moves narrative criticism away from being a purely reader-centered (pragmatic) type of criticism and makes it a more text-centered (objective) approach.

The scheme suggests other important implications. It provides, for instance, a basis for discussing what the reader knows. Unlike rhetorical criticism, narrative criticism does not interpret works from the perspective of the text's actual, original audience; it is not necessary to know everything they knew in order to understand the text aright. The implied reader, however, does know some things that are not stated in the text. For example, the implied reader of the Gospels surely knows that a talent is worth more than a denarius (the text assumes this), although real readers today might not have this knowledge. In other cases, the situation can be reversed. Real readers may find that they do have knowledge (e.g., information from the other Gospels) that the implied reader of a given narrative lacks. Such knowledge can spoil the intended effect of the story.

The goal of narrative criticism is to read the text as the implied reader. Kingsbury describes the implied reader as the "imaginary person in whom the intention of the text is to be thought of as always reaching its fulfillment."[27] To read in this way, it is necessary to know everything that the text assumes the reader knows and to "forget" everything that the text does not assume the reader knows. The critic should ask the questions that the text assumes its reader will ask but should not be distracted by questions that the implied reader would not ask.[28] The implied reader, furthermore, is not necessarily to be thought of as a first-time reader. In some instances the narrative text apparently assumes the reader will come to an understanding only after multiple readings.[29]

Some reader-response critics object to the concept of an implied reader employed in narrative criticism. They argue that the concept is inattentive to certain hermeneutical realities. No actual reader would ever be able to grasp all the complex interrelationships that may occur within a text. Descriptions of ideal implied readers, furthermore, are always offered by actual readers and will inevitably reflect the particular interests or conditioning of the latter.

20

Discussion concerning this hermeneutical circle will no doubt continue to play a significant part in the ongoing dialogue between narrative critics and reader-response scholars. For now, it is important to stress that in narrative criticism the implied reader is a hypothetical concept: it is not necessary to assume that such a person actually existed or ever could exist. To the extent that the implied reader is an idealized abstraction, the goal of reading the text "as the implied reader" may be somewhat unattainable, but it remains a worthy goal nevertheless. The concept is actually a principle that sets criteria for interpretation. With regard to any proposed reading, the question may be asked, Is there anything *in the text* that indicates the reader is expected to respond in this way? Narrative critics consider this question worth asking, even if it is not always possible to obtain an absolutely certain or perfectly clear answer.

These matters may seem trivial to a beginner, and ultimately that perception could prove correct. In recent years, narrative criticism and reader-response criticism have been coming closer together. Iser also employs a concept of an implied reader, though he defines this as a construct of the real reader's interaction with the text rather than as a construct of the implied author that lies within the text itself. Nevertheless, Booth now speaks of the implied reader in both senses and stresses the need to consider the effect of "authorial silence" on the reader, a notion reminiscent of Iser's attention to "gaps."[30] Of all the types of literary criticism discussed in this chapter, narrative criticism and the dialectical modes ("with" the text) of reader-response are the most similar and they may eventually become indistinguishable.

3

Story and Discourse

As its name implies, narrative criticism is concerned with a particular type of literature. A *narrative* may be defined as any work of literature that tells a story. This is a broad definition, but it is not all-inclusive. Other schools of literary criticism, for example, are devoted to the study of essays or poetry. In the New Testament, the four Gospels and Acts qualify as narratives. The epistles probably do not.[1]

Narratives have two aspects: story and discourse.[2] *Story* refers to the content of the narrative, what it is about. A story consists of such elements as events, characters, and settings, and the interaction of these elements comprises what we call the plot. *Discourse* refers to the rhetoric of the narrative, how the story is told. Stories concerning the same basic events, characters, and settings can be told in ways that produce very different narratives. The four Gospels provide excellent examples of this.

Narrative criticism is interested in what Chatman calls "story-as-discoursed."[3] A central question is, How does the implied author guide the implied reader in understanding the story? Narrative critics tend to think that the reader is guided through devices intrinsic to the process of storytelling.

POINT OF VIEW

One way that the implied author influences the reader's apprehension of the text is by insisting that the reader adopt a point of view consistent with that of the narrative. The notion of *point of view* is a pervasive one in narrative criticism and we shall encounter it in other contexts. Here we are concerned with what scholars call the *evaluative*

23

point of view, which governs a work in general. This refers to the norms, values, and general worldview that the implied author establishes as operative for the story. To put it another way, evaluative point of view may be defined as the standards of judgment by which readers are led to evaluate the events, characters, and settings that comprise the story.

As readers, we must accept the implied author's evaluative point of view even if it means suspending our own judgments during the act of reading. We may have to accept the notion that cowboys are good and Indians are bad. We may have to believe in talking animals or flying spaceships. And even if we are atheists, we will have to become Christians for a while if we are to read Bunyan or Dante. Readers are free, of course, to critique the point of view a narrative espouses. An initial acceptance of that point of view, however, is essential as preliminary to such criticism, for without such acceptance the story can never be understood in the first place.

All four of the New Testament Gospels depict a world that includes supernatural beings and events. They also presuppose a particular ethical stance that, even when undefined, is certainly assumed. This stance takes the form of a basic distinction between truth and untruth: ways of thinking are seen as right or wrong. The right way of thinking, furthermore, is aligned with God's point of view. As Kingsbury puts it, the implied authors of these narratives have made God's evaluative point of view normative for their works. What God thinks is, by definition, true and right.[4]

How is God's evaluative point of view determined? In each narrative, God must be regarded as a figure in the story world and God's perspective must be defined in terms of how it is depicted by the implied author. Occasionally, God speaks and acts directly, just like the characters in the stories. At other times, God speaks through agents such as angels and prophets and is presumed to act through dreams and the working of events that would otherwise be inexplicable (e.g., Matt. 27:51-53; Mark 15:33, 38). The Gospels also make references and allusions to the Hebrew Scriptures, which apparently count as the word of God. The reader, then, is expected to accept not only that God's point of view is true and right, but also that God's point of view can be expressed reliably through angels, prophets, miracles, dreams, and Scripture.

The Gospels also allow for another way of thinking—one opposed to God's point of view. The implied authors might be said to establish a second perspective as normative for their narratives, namely, the evaluative point of view of Satan. This perspective is normative in a negative sense, insofar as it comprises what is wrong and untrue.[5] In the synoptic Gospels, Satan, like God, speaks and acts directly in the narratives and also works indirectly through agents, namely, the demons. Satan may work through human characters as well (Luke 22:3; John 8:44); in Matthew and Mark, thinking "like people" is specifically designated as expressive of Satan's point of view (Matt. 16:23; Mark 8:33). It has been suggested, then, that a central opposition in the Gospels is between "thinking the things of God" and "thinking the things of people."[6]

The creation of a narrative world in which God's evaluative point of view can be determined and must be accepted as normative is a powerful rhetorical device. It gives significant direction to the reader's interpretation of the story; the implied reader will tend to empathize with those characters who express God's point of view and will seek distance from those characters who do not. Thus, in the process of telling these stories, the implied authors provide standards that govern their interpretation.

NARRATION

Another way the implied author guides the reader is through the use of a narrator—the voice that the implied author uses to tell the story. Booth notes that one famous work of literature begins with the line, "There was a man in the land of Uz, whose name was Job; and that man was perfect and upright, one that feared God, and eschewed evil." This initial sentence shapes the reader's response to all that follows. The statement is incredible, yet is one that the reader accepts without question. In the real world, this would not be so. We would want to know whose opinion this is, and on what basis such claims are being made. The process of storytelling, however, may involve an implicit contract between author and reader in which the latter agrees to trust the narrator.[7]

Narrators differ in important respects. Some works have first-person narrators who may also be characters in the story. This is the case in Mark Twain's *Huckleberry Finn*. With few exceptions (Luke 1:3; John 1:14-16; 21:24), the narrators of our Gospels speak only in the third person and are not characters in the stories that they tell. In Acts, however, the narrator does at times appear to be a character (see the famous "we" passages: 16:10-17; 20:5-15; 21:1-18; 27:1—28:16).

25

Narrators also vary with regard to how much they know and how much they choose to tell. In all four Gospels, the narrators seem very knowledgeable. They are able to report not only public events, but also private ones in which a character is supposedly alone (e.g., Mark 14:32-42). They are able to tell us what happened in two different places at the same time (e.g., John 18:12-27). They even know the inner thoughts and motivations of the characters they describe (e.g., Matt. 2:3). Still, their knowledge may have limits. In the synoptic Gospels at least, the narrators' perceptions are limited spatially and temporally to the earthly realm. Descriptions of heaven and hell are offered only by characters in the stories, never by the narrators themselves. We do not find statements like those in the Old Testament that simply declare outright whether God is pleased or displeased with someone.[8] Rather, if God is pleased with somebody in these narratives, God enters the story and says so (Matt. 3:17; 17:5; Mark 1:11; Luke 3:22). The narrators may know the inner thoughts of Jesus, but, unlike Jesus, they do not presume to speak directly for God. In the Gospel of John, such restrictions are lessened: the narrator is able to describe the divine realm (1:1-5), and at times his point of view becomes indistinguishable from that of Jesus.[9] Furthermore, the narrator of John's Gospel claims to know far more than he tells (20:30; 21:25), an affirmation that emphasizes the extent to which the reader is dependent upon him.

Narrators are also described in terms of their reliability. Modern literature sometimes employs the device of an unreliable narrator, whose views the reader is expected to challenge or discount. The narrator of Ken Kesey's *One Flew Over the Cuckoo's Nest* is an insane man who sometimes confuses reality and fantasy. Most narrative critics, however, regard the Gospels as having reliable narrators whose points of view are in perfect accord with those of the implied authors. The reader is expected to believe everything that these narrators say. When the narrator of Matthew's Gospel says that John the Baptist is "the one spoken of by the prophet" (3:3), the implied reader does not question whether this is actually true.[10]

Some narrators are more intrusive than others. In certain works, as in Thornton Wilder's drama *Our Town*, the narrator is present in a very obvious way, providing explicit commentary on the story as it develops. The narrators of our Gospels are generally less conspicuous, but occasionally they too burst the bounds of the story and address the reader explicitly (Mark 13:14; John 20:31).

According to narrative critics, there is always a narrator, though at times this device is used so subtly that it may almost go unnoticed. Similarly, it is always possible to speak of a "narratee" to whom the story is being told. In Luke-Acts the story is ostensibly being told to someone named Theophilus (Luke 1:3; Acts 1:1), and the implied reader is simply invited to listen in on the telling. In other works, the narratee is not explicitly identified, but the reader still senses that he or she is overhearing a story being told to someone.

The communication model for narrative criticism, then, can be expanded as follows:

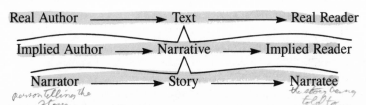

Real Author ⟶ Text ⟶ Real Reader

Implied Author ⟶ Narrative ⟶ Implied Reader

Narrator ⟶ Story ⟶ Narratee

The narrator and the narratee are not identical with the implied author and the implied reader. They are rhetorical devices, created by the implied author. They are part of the narrative itself, part of the discourse through which the story is told.[11]

It should also be noted that levels of narration can sometimes be observed within a literary work, so that the model diagrammed above could be extended still further. The parables of Jesus found within our Gospels are excellent examples of this for they are, in effect, stories within stories. In analyzing the parable of the Good Samaritan (Luke 10:25-37), Jesus himself might be identified as the narrator and the lawyer to whom he tells the story might be identified as the narratee. On another level, however, both Jesus and the lawyer may be identified as characters in a story being told to Theophilus by an unnamed narrator.

SYMBOLISM AND IRONY

Sometimes the implied author of a literary work encourages the reader to reject certain interpretations and to accept or at least try out alternative ones. Symbolism and irony are useful rhetorical devices for accomplishing this purpose.

It is possible to misread a narrative by taking every word and phrase literally. An article in a recent medical journal attempts to interpret Luke 22:44 by explaining how a rare type of hemorrhage

27

could have caused Jesus, under stress, to lose blood through his sweat glands.[12] It is extremely unlikely, however, that the implied reader of Luke's narrative would think Jesus was hemorrhaging in the garden of Gethsemane. Rather, the narrator's observation that Jesus' sweat became "like great drops of blood" is a simile, a common figure of speech that is no more intended to be read literally than Jesus' comparison of himself to a mother hen elsewhere in this story (Luke 13:34).

As if to guard against such readings, the Gospel narratives contain accounts that lampoon the literally minded. A well-known story in Mark's Gospel has Jesus' disciples foolishly thinking his warning to beware of the "leaven" of the religious leaders means that they should not purchase bread or yeast from them (Mark 8:14-21; cf. Matt. 16:5-12). The Gospel of John is replete with such misunderstandings. Nicodemus thinks he must reenter the womb of his mother in order to be "born again" (3:4). Jesus tells his disciples that Lazarus has "fallen asleep" and they assume the latter is enjoying a restful nap (11:12). Jesus tells them, "I have food that you know not of," and they wonder who has been sneaking him provisions (4:33). When he says, "Where I am going, you cannot come," people think he plans to commit suicide (8:21-22), and when he speaks of his flesh as "bread for the life of this world," they believe he is advocating some bizarre form of cannibalism (6:51-52). Culpepper has indicated that the purpose of reporting these frequent misunderstandings is to teach the reader how to read the Gospel.[13] The initial false assumptions of characters are often corrected through comments by the narrator or by Jesus himself that provide a more appropriate interpretation. At other times, the right understanding is not spelled out and the reader must struggle to learn the significance of phrases like "bread of life" and "living water." In any case, the reader realizes that, in this narrative, there is often more than meets the eye. The reader becomes sensitized to the detection of multiple meanings and looks for possible instances of symbolism even where no misunderstanding has occurred. The seamless robe of Christ (19:23), the unbroken net of fishes (21:6, 8, 11), the water and blood that flow from Jesus' side (19:34)—do these references also have significance that is more than literal?

Literary theorists sometimes distinguish between such literary devices as figures of speech (e.g., similes and metaphors), images, signs, symbols, and motifs. What all of these conventions have in common, however, is the establishment of some special communion between the implied author and the implied reader, through which the latter is guided to a particular understanding of the narrative. In every instance, what is said means more than it appears to mean, so that the reader must persist to find the true or at least advanced understanding. Animals such as doves, pigs, serpents, or lambs may function as symbols. Numbers can have symbolic significance. Sometimes entire actions or events are symbolic; a woman's anointing of Jesus signifies his preparation for burial (Mark 14:3-9). Settings such as mountains, deserts, weddings, and feasts are fraught with symbolic meaning.

The implied author provides through symbolism what Culpepper calls "implicit commentary and directional signals" for the reader.[14] The problem for narrative critics, however, is recognizing what the symbols mean. It is easy for interpreters to get carried away in their explanations of symbolism, as any survey of theories on the significance of the "153 fish" of John 21:11 will clearly attest. The goal of narrative criticism must be to uncover the meaning intended by the implied author, a meaning that is not esoteric but that the implied reader is expected to grasp.

Philip Wheelwright has suggested four categories from which the meanings of symbols may be derived.[15]

1. *Archetypal symbols* derive their meaning from contexts that are virtually universal, such as the basic opposition of light and darkness.
2. *Symbols of ancestral vitality* derive their meaning from earlier sources. In our Gospels, these include images drawn from the Old Testament: the wilderness as a place of testing, the number 12 as suggestive of Israel, and so on.
3. *Symbols created by the implied author* can be understood only within the context of the particular narrative. The reader of Mark's Gospel, for example, may be led to identify the withered fig tree (11:12-24) as a symbol of Israel's obsolete temple cult.
4. *Symbols of cultural range* derive their meaning from the social and historical context of the real author and his or her community.

This fourth type of symbol poses a special problem for narrative critics: access to the meaning of these symbols is not gained through the narrative itself, for the implied author simply assumes the reader will understand them. If modern critics are to read the narrative as the implied reader they must at this point rely on insights gained from historical criticism. What does Jesus mean when he calls Herod "a fox"

(Luke 13:32)? In the modern world, a person who is called a fox might be thought of as sly, cunning, or deceitful. A survey of ancient literature, however, reveals that at the time of Luke's writing, foxes were more likely to be viewed as rapacious and destructive. Furthermore, foxes are often presented in literature of the period as a threat to chickens, an image that is especially telling since it is in this same passage that Jesus goes on to compare himself to a mother hen (13:34).[16]

Another concept that has received much attention in biblical studies is the literary technique of irony. Symbolism and irony are related insofar as both involve a detection of multiple meanings. Symbolism, however, implies a recognition that something means more than it initially appears to mean, while irony implies that the true interpretation is actually contrary to the apparent meaning. The woman's anointing of Jesus with nard (Mark 14:3-9) is symbolic because it signifies not only her act of affection but also his preparation for burial. The soldiers' crowning of Jesus with thorns (Mark 15:17), on the other hand, is ironic, for what is intended as ridicule actually pays peculiar homage to the king who reigns through suffering.

Boris Uspensky defines irony as a "nonconcurrence" of point of view as revealed through speech, actions, motives, or beliefs.[17] A character's speech may be recognized as ironic, for example, if the point of view expressed does not concur with that of the character's actions. When the soldiers hail Jesus as "King of the Jews," strike him with a reed, and spit upon him (Mark 15:18-19), their speech presents a point of view incongruous with what is expressed by their actions. Similarly, actions might be recognized as ironic if they do not concur with motives, and so on. In its most basic sense, then, irony is "always the result of a disparity of understanding."[18]

Some scholars distinguish between *verbal irony* and *situational irony*. Verbal irony refers to instances in which the speaker intentionally says one thing, but means another. Situational (or dramatic) irony, on the other hand, contains what D. C. Mueke calls an element of "unawareness."[19] In situational irony, people are unwitting victims; they are not aware that they are being ironical. A classic instance of such irony occurs in John 11:49-52, when Caiaphas declares that Jesus will die "for the people." The implied reader recognizes this as a testimony to the triumphant and saving effect of Jesus' death, though of course the character of Caiaphas in John's Gospel does not intend for his words to be interpreted in this way, nor is he aware that they might be.

30

In the example just cited, the irony is obvious, for the narrator draws the reader's attention to it in a way that is hard to miss. Sometimes, however, irony is used in ways that are more covert. Booth stresses that irony must be discovered by the reader.[20] Since by its very nature irony tends toward subtlety, it cannot always be recognized and interpreted with precision. There is always the possibility of missing it. On the other hand, as Paul Duke puts it, "Scholars and critics who quest after ironies in a text are prone, once they have caught the thrill of the hunt, to become downright intoxicated, not only bagging their limit so to speak, but opening fire on everything in the text that moves."[21] Accordingly, some discussions of what is to be perceived as ironic tend to reveal more about the creativity of the critic than about that of the author.

In spite of such pitfalls, attention to irony is essential to narrative criticism. Our Gospels are filled with ironic moments. In Luke, a Pharisee thanks God he is not like a certain tax collector without realizing it is the latter whom God considers justified (18:9-14). In Mark, James and John ask to be placed at Jesus' right and left (10:35-40), not knowing these positions will be occupied by people on crosses (15:27). In fact, the basic story lines of our Gospels are built upon extended ironies: the people of Israel reject their Messiah; God's own Son is accused of blasphemy by characters who are themselves blasphemers; people opposed to God serve as unwitting instruments in bringing God's will to pass.[22] Such ironies are rooted in a theme found in all four Gospel narratives, namely, the idea that God's rule comes in ways that people do not expect.[23]

Both irony and symbolism are rhetorical devices through which the implied author guides the reader in interpreting the story. Booth lists four steps through which such guidance takes place: The reader (1) rejects the literal meaning of the words in response to internal or external clues,[24] (2) tries out alternative explanations, (3) evaluates these in terms of what he or she believes about the implied author, and (4) makes a decision based on the assumed intentions of the author.[25] These stages of reconstruction may all occur in an instant, but even so the process forces the reader into a brief encounter with the implied author. In order to make sense of the text, the reader must not only consider the implied author's intentions but, ultimately, adopt them.

For this reason, symbolism and irony are powerful rhetorical devices. Their use presents the reader with at least two levels of meaning and an invitation to "come and live at a higher" location. In working through these stages of reconstruction the reader makes what Booth calls "a delightful leap of intuition."[26] To grasp what others have missed can be inherently gratifying; the reader sees what characters in the story fail to see. Thus, irony bonds the reader to the implied author through persuasion that "rests on implicit flattery."[27] In addition to this winsome aspect, other effects have been observed by biblical scholars. Duke notes that "irony rewards its followers with a sense of community."[28] Since it is possible to miss the intended meaning in irony (or in symbolism), recognition of that meaning offers readers a shared experience of like-mindedness. Furthermore, Culpepper observes that the use of irony and symbolism encourages repeated readings of a narrative because "even the most perceptive reader is never sure he or she has received all the signals the text is sending."[29]

NARRATIVE PATTERNS

The implied author may also guide the reader in understanding the text through the use of *narrative patterns*. Such patterns are often difficult to define, but they include recurrent structural devices and design features that are used to organize and present the story. In a basic sense, these include the arrangement of the text into sentences, paragraphs, and chapters. In modern editions of the Bible, however, patterns of this sort may reflect the decisions of translators rather than the intentions of the implied author. For example, the system of chapters and verses so familiar to Bible readers today is a modern imposition on the text. While facilitating reference, it is in no way definitive of the patterns that are found within the narratives themselves.

Narrative critics are more interested in discerning literary principles that the implied author follows in organizing the work. Such an interest is not new; in biblical studies, identification of organizational motifs has been part of composition analysis and rhetorical criticism for some time. As a result, narrative critics find there is a wealth of information already available on this important aspect of literary study.

David Bauer has modified systems developed by Robert Traina and Howard Kuist to propose 15 categories of "compositional relationships" found in biblical narrative.[30]

1. *Repetition* involves a recurrence of similar or identical elements. John 18 Peters Denial 3 times   John 21 Jesus Ask Peter Do you love m 3 times
2. *Contrast* associates or juxtaposes things that are dissimilar or opposite. The beloved disciple. unwavering faith and loyality Disciples Peter denies 3x + desserts Jesus.

32

3. *Comparison* associates or juxtaposes things that are alike or similar. 2 John-Cana wedding feast Mary They have no wine) statement 4 John-Soldier My son is dieing Does not Ask

4. *Causation and Substantiation* order the narrative through Act 2:13-36 relationships of cause and effect (causation is the movement from cause to effect and substantiation, from effect to cause.)

5. *Climax* represents a movement from lesser to greater intensity. John 11 Jesus Raises Lazarus from the dead. cause for Jesus put to death

6. *Pivot* involves a change in the direction of the material, either Act 9. conversion of from positive developments to negative ones or vice versa. Paul.

1 S3-8 ~~7.~~ *Particularization and Generalization* involve movement in the text toward explication that becomes either more specific or more comprehensive.

8. *Statements of purpose* structure the narrative according to a movement from means to end. John 9 Disciples ask who sinned. Jesus gives purpose show God ed power

9. *Preparation* refers to the inclusion of material in one part of the narrative that serves primarily to prepare the reader for what is still to come. John 12 Mary of Bethany annoints Jesus feet, next chapter Jesus washes the disciples feet

10. *Summarization* offers a synopsis or abridgement of material that is treated more fully elsewhere.

11. *Interrogation* is the employment of a question or problem followed by its answer or solution. John 9

12. *Inclusio* refers to a repetition of features at the beginning and end of a unit, as exemplified by the use of antiphons in liturgical poetry (cf. Ps. 8:1, 9). start with something end with something

13. *Interchange* involves an alternation of elements in an "a, b, a, b" pattern. (In Luke 1–2, the narrative alternates between nativity stories dealing with John the Baptist and ones dealing with Jesus).

14. *Chiasm* has to do with a repetition of elements in an inverted order: "a, b, b, a" (e.g., the elements evil/good/righteous/unrighteous in Matt. 5:45).

15. *Intercalation* refers to the insertion of one literary unit in the midst of another. Mark 5:21-43 miracle within another miracle story.

Narrative critics are interested in these compositional patterns for what they reveal about the implied author. Rhoads and Michie identify particularization as "the most pervasive stylistic feature of Mark's Gospel": statements such as, "The time is fulfilled and the kingdom of God is at hand" (1:15) offer the reader a general comment followed by a more precise formulation of the same idea.[31] In fact, Mark liked this

33

device so much that he related a story that provides a paradigm for how it works (8:22-25). Mark is also fond of arranging entire episodes in a chiastic pattern,[32] and his Gospel provides some of the best examples of intercalation in all literature (5:21-43; 11:12-25). Other narratives exhibit different patterns. The book of Acts seems to be organized according to a principle of generalization (1:8). Within the book, Peter's speeches often take the form of substantiation, explaining what is behind something that has just transpired: the abnormal behavior of the disciples on Pentecost (2:14-36), the healing of a cripple (3:12-26; 4:8-12), or the baptism of Gentiles (11:1-18). The conversion of Saul in Acts 9 is a classic example of a positive pivot.

All of these patterns can apply to narrative units of various sizes and lengths, from individual sentences to paragraphs or entire books. They are intrinsic to the practice of storytelling. In fact, as Bauer indicates, relationships such as these are rooted in art. They may be found in music, painting, sculpture, and architecture, as well as in non-narrative forms of literature.[33] Whether they were aware of it or not, each of our Gospel writers chose to tell his story of Jesus in one way rather than another. Decisions were made about how to organize and arrange the material and these decisions inevitably affect the reader's apprehension of the tale.

4

Events

Every story encompasses three elements: events, characters, and settings. Somebody does something to someone, somewhere, at some time. The "something" that is done is an event, the "somebody" and "someone" are characters, and the "somewhere" and "sometime" are settings.

Events, then, are the incidents or happenings that occur within a story, and a story cannot exist without them. Seymour Chatman notes that the statement, "Peter had no friends or relatives" is not a story, for it does not describe an event. Such statements as "Peter died" and "Only one person came to Peter's funeral" do describe events and may be considered (either separately or in combination) as comprising a story.[1]

We should be careful not to think of events too narrowly, in the limited sense of physical action. In the past, such a conception has resulted in a false dichotomy between "narrative material" and "sayings material" in the Gospels. Chatman stresses that events may include speech ("John said, 'I'm hungry' "), thoughts ("John thought that he would go") or even feelings and perceptions ("John felt uneasy").[2] Accordingly, the speeches and sayings of Jesus reported in the Gospels are themselves events and should be considered part of the narrative.

A NARRATIVE UNDERSTANDING OF EVENTS

Simply to consider events as the content of a narrative or as definitive of what we have called the story is not enough. One must also consider the "story-as-discoursed," the manner in which the events are presented by the implied author.

35

Kernels and Satellites

Roland Barthes has observed that not all events are of equal importance.[3] Some events, called *kernels*, are so essential that they could not possibly be removed without destroying the logic of the narrative. Others, called *satellites*, could conceivably be deleted without disturbing the basic plot. The narrative would still make sense, although its effectiveness or aesthetic quality might be diminished. Barthes believes that the kernels, once identified, should reveal a logical progression of contingency. In other words, kernel events are those in which choices are made that determine the subsequent development of the narrative. Satellite events do not involve choices but simply describe the working-out of those choices made at the kernels.

While granting the basic idea of some hierarchy in the significance of events, biblical scholars have not made much use of this concept of kernels and satellites. This is probably because, in spite of Barthes' suggestions, there seem to be few objective criteria for making such determinations. It seems strange, then, that Chatman is impressed with "how easily consensus is reached about which are the kernels and which are the satellites of a given story." He believes the distinction is "a psychological reality that anyone can prove."[4] This has certainly not been the case in biblical studies, where scholars have found such distinctions to be anything but self-evident.

Order

Gerard Genette and others have called attention to temporal relations that govern the reporting of events in literature.[5] An important distinction is made between *story time* and *discourse time*. Story time refers to the order in which events are conceived to have occurred by the implied author in creating the world of the story. Discourse time refers to the order in which the events are described for the reader by the narrator. Sometimes the narrator of a story may jump ahead in time to tell the reader what is going to happen later or drop back to describe something that has already occurred. In Matthew, for example, the reader is not told about the murder of John the Baptist until 14:1-2. Suddenly, Herod speculates as to whether Jesus might be John raised from the dead. Only then does the narrator go on to explain in some detail how Herod had John executed (14:3-12). The reader realizes that this event is being reported out of sequence, that it actually occurred earlier in story time. The implied author could, of course, have the narrator report all events in their exact chronological order, but this would be less interesting and ultimately less effective. The order in which events are reported is an important part of a narrative's discourse, of how a story is told.

Discrepancies between the order of events in story time and discourse time are called *anachronies.* Narrative critics sometimes describe different types of anachronies with categories that can be mentioned only briefly here.[6] A general distinction is made between *analepses,* in which an event is narrated belatedly, and *prolepses,* in which an event is narrated prematurely. The account of John's death in Matthew 14 is an analepsis. True prolepses seem not to occur in our Gospels, in the sense of events that are fully narrated before they actually occur. Biblical scholars, however, often use this term in an expanded sense to include predictions and forecasts concerning events still to come.

Analepses and prolepses may be described as either *internal* or *external,* depending on whether they lie within the temporal parameters of the story. The narrator of Matthew's Gospel, for instance, tells a story that begins with Jesus' birth and ends with his resurrection. The account of John's death in Matthew 14 is therefore an internal analepsis because it is presumed to have occurred during the time period covered by this story. On the other hand, Matthew's recollections of what ancient prophets said are external analepses because they recall events that transpired before this story about Jesus began. Scholars who regard predictions as prolepses would class the predictions of Jesus' death and resurrection in Matthew as internal prolepses and the predictions of his second coming as external prolepses, since only the former are fulfilled within the story. Thus we see that, although the story of Matthew's Gospel deals with a sequence of events from Jesus' birth to his resurrection, this story is told from a temporal perspective that can reach all the way back to creation (19:4, 8; 24:21; 25:34) or forward to the "close of the age" (13:49; 24:3; 28:20).

Mixed anachronies occur only partially within story time. The Gospel of John contains numerous mixed analepses, where events that began prior to the commencement of events narrated in the story are described as continuing into story time (e.g., 8:58, "Before Abraham was, I am"). The Gospel of Matthew does not contain any mixed analepses of this sort because, in Matthew's narrative, the story of Jesus is not continuous with that of Israel.[7] On the other hand, Matthew does contain mixed prolepses, which indicate that the story of Jesus is continuous with that of his followers (cf. 18:20; 28:20).

Duration

The amount of time that the narrator devotes to reporting an event may be radically inconsistent with the amount of time that is assumed to have transpired in the story during the event's occurence. Genette has defined five different ways in which the duration of discourse time may be related to that of story time.[8]

1. *Summary* refers to instances when discourse time is briefer than story time. The reader perceives that the event took longer to transpire within the world of the story than it takes for the narrator to report it. The narrator of Luke's Gospel covers several years of Jesus' life in one sentence: "The child grew and became strong" (2:41).

2. *Scene* refers to instances when the duration of discourse time and story time are roughly equivalent. The reader realizes that it takes the narrator about the same amount of time to report the event as it would have taken for the event to have actually occurred within the story. Speeches and the reporting of direct discourse provide the best examples, but sometimes a detailed blow-by-blow account of actions may qualify as a scene.

3. *Stretch* refers to instances when story time is briefer than discourse time, a phenomenon that does not seem to occur in biblical narrative. In modern literature, a narrator may devote pages to describing a thought, perception, or inner feeling of a character that, in terms of story time, transpired in a moment. The narrators of our Gospels do not do this, and, for this reason, their stories move along more quickly than most modern novels.

4. *Ellipsis* refers to instances when discourse time stops while story time continues. The reader must assume that time has continued to pass within the story world even though the narrator does not report it. In our Gospels, ellipses frequently occur between episodes. For example, in Mark 1:32-34, the narrator reports that Jesus healed many people one evening. In Mark 1:35, the narrator reports what Jesus does in the morning. The reader assumes that several hours have passed in the world of the story, even though the discourse of the narrative does not report this.

5. *Pause* refers to instances when story time stops while discourse time continues. The narrator takes "time out" to describe or explain

something to the reader and then picks up the story again where he or she left off. The reader perceives that no time has passed in the world of the story while this special explanation or description was being given. A good example of pause is found in Mark 7:3-4, where the narrator brings the story of Jesus' conflict with the Pharisees to a halt long enough to provide some background information that will help the reader interpret the event.

Classification of such references is not an end in itself, since the goal of narrative criticism is to interpret the work as a whole. What narrative critics hope to gain from application of Genette's categories is a means of gauging the pace of the narrative, of determining where it speeds up and where it slows down.

Frequency

Narrative critics are also interested in the frequency with which events occur in a story and in the frequency with which they are reported. Genette describes four possible relationships between frequency in discourse time and story time.[9]

1. *Singular narration* reports once an event that happens once. This is the most common and natural means of telling a story.

2. *Repetitive narration* reports repeatedly an event that happens once. This may be illustrated by the three accounts of Paul's Damascus road experience in Acts. The reader does not imagine that Paul has had such an experience three times, but realizes it is the same event being described, first by the narrator (9:1-9) and then by Paul himself (22:4-16; 26:9-18).

3. *Multiple-singular narration* reports repeatedly an event that happens repeatedly. An example can be found in Matthew, where there are two accounts of religious leaders asking Jesus for a sign (12:38-45; 16:1-4). The reader realizes that these are two separate, albeit similar occurrences.

4. *Iterative narration* reports once an event that happens repeatedly. An example can be found in Luke 22:39, where the narrator tells us that Jesus went "as was his custom to the Mount of Olives." The reader realizes from this single narrative reference that the event of Jesus going to the Mount of Olives has occurred many times.

The frequency with which events are referred to in the telling of a story is important to narrative criticism because it affects the reader's understanding of the narrative as a whole. Repetition usually implies some type of emphasis, for it requires the reader to consider the significance of an event more than once. By controlling frequency of reference to events, the implied author is able to send signals to the reader that offer guidance in making sense of the text.

Causation

To understand the plot of a narrative, it is also important to recognize elements of causality that link events to each other. Causal relationships between events may be subdivided into categories of *possibility, probability,* and *contingency.* Only in the latter case can one event actually be said to *cause* another. The first category refers to instances when an event simply makes possible the occurrence of another. Relationships of probability, likewise, are those in which one event makes the occurrence of another more likely.

E. M. Forster has argued that causality is a definitive characteristic of plot.[10] A statement such as, "The king died and then the queen died," does not constitute a plot because it merely records two unrelated events and tells us the order in which they happened. In order for a story to have a plot, the events must be related to each other in some meaningful fashion. More often than not, this is accomplished by introducing the element of causation. According to Forster, "The king died and then the queen died *of grief*" is a plot, because a causal link has been established between the events.

Chatman pushes Forster's argument a step further.[11] The principle of causation is so strong in literature, Chatman suggests, that the reader expects it and will in fact infer it even when it is not stated. Unless otherwise instructed, a reader who encounters Forster's first statement, "The king died and then the queen died," will assume that the two events are related and that the king's death in some way precipitates that of the queen. The two statements proposed by Forster differ only in the degree of explicitness with which the causal link is spelled out. The element of causation is present, or will be assumed to be present, in both.[12]

These insights regarding the principle of causation have significance for a literary reading of our Gospels. All four Gospels have plots that are basically *episodic.*[13] The stories consist of brief incidents or episodes that are reported one right after another. In many cases, these episodes may be understood and appreciated apart from the rest of the narrative. Nevertheless, a literary reading will expect to find causal links between them, links that may be explicitly stated or simply implied.

To demonstrate how such a principle may be applied in narrative criticism, let us consider a selected passage from Matthew's Gospel. In Matt. 12:9-14, we read about Jesus entering a synagogue on the Sabbath and encountering a man with a withered hand. Some of the Pharisees watch him closely. They ask him, "Is it lawful to heal on the Sabbath?" so that they might accuse him. Jesus responds to their question, affirming that it is lawful "to do good on the Sabbath," and then heals the man. The narrator concludes the episode by noting that the Pharisees "went out and took counsel against him, how to destroy him." The narrator does not say that the Pharisees do this on account of what has just happened in the synagogue but the reader will certainly infer such a causal link. Thus, the importance of this passage in Matthew's Gospel is not limited to what insight it offers concerning the relative ethical value of Sabbath laws and deeds of mercy. It is important for an understanding of the narrative as a whole because it provides the immediate motivation for the introduction of the plot to kill Jesus, which will be a major concern in the story from this point on.

The reader who is familiar with Matthew's Gospel may be somewhat surprised by the foregoing analysis because, as the story develops, the incident concerning the man with the withered hand does not come up again. When Jesus is finally brought to trial, he is not sentenced to death for healing on the Sabbath, but for blasphemy, that is, for claiming to possess divine authority. This apparent contradiction is resolved, however, when it is recognized that Matt. 12:9-14 is also linked causally to the episode that precedes it. The first eight verses of Matthew 12 recount a prior incident between Jesus and the Pharisees, one that also involves the Sabbath law. Jesus is challenged for allowing his disciples to pick grain on the Sabbath and he responds by claiming that he, the Son of man, is "lord of the Sabbath." It is this claim that explains why, later the same day, the Pharisees watch Jesus so closely when he enters the synagogue. It also explains why they have already determined to accuse him even before the controversial healing takes place. In fact, the incident involving the man with the withered hand appears to be simply a "test case" for the Pharisees, by which they seek to discern whether Jesus really meant what he said in their previous encounter. Accordingly, although the plot to kill Jesus is immediately linked to his healing on the Sabbath, this event is itself linked to something more substantive, namely, his claim to be one who has

41

authority over the Sabbath. Such a claim would be interpreted by the religious leaders as blasphemous.

The perception of causal links between episodes in the Gospels is a feature of narrative criticism new to biblical studies. Under the dominance of historical criticism, the Gospels were usually treated as collections of various pericopes that were not intrinsically related to each other. Even when attention was paid to the compositional arrangement of these pericopes in their current context, the emphasis was usually on detecting topical or merely sequential relationships between units. Narrative criticism, however, looks for logical progressions of cause and effect.

Such perceptions, of course, may be taken too far and causal relationships that are strained or farfetched might be suggested. It would not be right to impose upon the Gospels the sort of deterministic plot structure found in some literature, where every event leads directly to another until the final outcome is inevitable.[14] Still, when it is possible to discern causal links that are sensible, the implied reader is likely to do so. As Chatman says, "our minds inveterately seek structure and will provide it if necessary."[15] There is an inherent tendency for readers to infer a principle of causation whenever and wherever it helps the narrative to make sense.

Conflict

In addition to the matters already discussed in this chapter, it is important to understand events in terms of conflict analysis. Laurence Perrine defines conflict broadly as "a clash of actions, ideas, desires, or wills."[16] Such oppositions seem to be integral to narrative, for it is difficult to imagine a story that does not contain some elements of conflict. Narrative critics are interested in defining such conflicts and in determining the manner in which they are developed and resolved.

Conflict may occur at various levels. Most common, perhaps, is conflict between characters, which can usually be defined in terms of inconsistent points of view or incompatible character traits. These matters will be discussed in more detail in chapter 5, but we should note that this is only one form that conflict can take. Perrine observes that conflict can also exist between characters and settings, that is, between people and their environment. Characters may also be presented as being in conflict with nature or with society or with "fate." For that matter, they may even be in conflict with themselves.[17]

Even a cursory reading of the Gospels reveals how pervasive the theme of conflict is in these narratives. Jesus encounters opposition not only from the religious leaders of Israel but also from his own disciples. At other times, he must subdue demonic forces and overcome powers of disease and death. He does battle with nature itself, stilling storms and walking on water. He agonizes and struggles within himself concerning his own destiny. And in the background, in all four Gospel stories, is the continual conflict between truth and untruth, between the things of God and the things of people.

The individual events that comprise a story may be analyzed in terms of what they contribute to the development and resolution of conflict in the narrative as a whole. The nature of conflict can sometimes be understood in terms of *threats* that parties pose to each other. As conflict develops in a narrative, its nature may change: a new threat may be added or an existing one removed. On the other hand, the essence of the conflict may remain the same, changing only in intensity.

The events described in Matt. 12:1-8 (picking grain on the Sabbath) and 12:9-14 (healing the man with a withered hand) help to define the conflict between Jesus and the religious leaders in Matthew's Gospel. The leaders are opposed to Jesus because they perceive him as posing a threat to the authority and sanctity of the law, particularly (in this case) the Sabbath law. This marks a new development in the conflict between Jesus and the leaders. Up to now, their opposition to him has not been defined in terms of a threat to the law. It is noteworthy, therefore, that in this same episode the leaders' threat to Jesus' life is brought into the narrative for the first time.[18]

This notion of threats should not be pressed too far in definition of conflict, since there are cases where it does not seem to apply. Jesus and his disciples have conflicts with each other in all four Gospels, but it may be difficult to think of them as posing threats to one another. Nevertheless, when such threats are present, it may be possible to describe resolution of conflict in terms of how they turn out. The threats may be fulfilled or they may be resolved in nonfulfillment. Conflict may also be left unresolved within a narrative. When this is the case, the effect can be highly significant, for unresolved conflict tends to impinge most directly on the reader. Readers expect and insist upon resolution to the point that, if the implied author does not provide it, they are likely to appropriate the conflict into their own lives and attempt to resolve it themselves. Most of us have seen films or read novels that left loose ends and we know that loose ends stay with us the longest. We wonder what we would have done if we had been in the character's place: How would we have resolved the conflict and what might have happened as a result?

One of the greatest instances of unresolved conflict in all literature is found in Luke 15:11-32, the story of the prodigal son. This classic tale ends with the older son being invited to put aside his pride and attend the joyful banquet that has been prepared in his brother's honor. The story, however, does not tell us if the boy accepts this invitation, and as a result it is almost impossible for the reader not to respond by asking, What would I do if I were he? The abrupt ending to the Gospel of Mark should probably be understood in the same way: the disciples, who have failed Jesus, are invited to come back to him. Mark, however, does not go on to narrate an actual reunion between Jesus and his disciples (as do Matthew, Luke, and John). The reader is left to imagine whether this reunion actually occurred and what such a reunion would be like. Most readers, it is assumed, will do so in terms relevant to their own experience.[19]

CASE STUDY: THE PLOT OF MATTHEW

A number of literary concepts important for the analysis of events have been defined and illustrated in this chapter. We will now seek to determine what light, if any, the application of these concepts can shed on the question, What is the plot of Matthew's Gospel?[20]

Kernels and Satellites in Matthew

Frank Matera tries to discover which events in Matthew's story are the kernels and which are the satellites.[21] Matera finds six kernel events, so designated because they represent turning points in the story. The birth of Jesus (2:1) introduces the crisis of how people will respond to the coming of the Messiah. The beginning of Jesus' ministry (4:12-17) represents a turning point in that this crisis now becomes more focused; the material that follows concentrates specifically on how Israel responds to Jesus' work of preaching, teaching, and healing. The question of John the Baptist (11:2-6) introduces material in which it is Jesus himself who must make a crucial decision. Faced with rejection by those to whom he has been sent, he determines that he will turn his attention to his own disciples and to any who will believe, even if they are Gentiles. Once this decision has been made, the conversation

44

at Caesarea Philippi (16:13-28) introduces the next crisis in the narrative. It now falls to Jesus' disciples to decide if they are willing to follow a Messiah who calls them to suffering and death. The fifth kernel, Jesus' cleansing of the temple (21:1-17), introduces the story of Jesus' passion and resurrection. Finally, the great commission is a kernel without satellites, serving both as the climax of the entire Gospel and as the introduction of a new crux to be faced by the reader: Will the Gospel be preached to all nations?

Matera's analysis is impressive, but not definitive. One might identify other significant turning points in the narrative, such as the introduction of the plot to kill Jesus in 12:14. It is also questionable whether the crucifixion and resurrection of Jesus should be viewed as satellites of the temple cleansing rather than as kernel events in their own right. How does one biblical scholar convince others that his or her selection of kernels is correct? To get around such an impasse it is necessary to consider the question of plot from other angles.

Order, Duration, and Frequency in Matthew

With regard to distinctions between story time and discourse time, two sets of events in Matthew's Gospel deserve special mention. First, the great speeches that Jesus gives are remarkable for the amount of discourse time devoted to them.[22] These are the premier examples of what Genette calls scenes, instances in which the duration of the discourse slows to approximate the actual expenditure of time in the story. Second, the events that comprise Matthew's passion narrative are presented in ways that make them stand out from the rest of the Gospel. Once again, the duration of discourse time slows considerably, such that Matthew spends three entire chapters (26–28) reporting the events of a single week. In addition, these events are the subject of most of the anachronies in Matthew's narrative. Jesus' passion is explicitly predicted through internal prolepses (16:21; 17:22-23; 20:17-19) and is alluded to many times (e.g., 9:15; 17:9-12). It is also foreshadowed in the slaughter of the Bethlehem infants (2:16-18) and in the murder of John the Baptist (14:1-12; cf. 17:12). Thus, frequency of reference and slowing of discourse time encourage the reader of Matthew's Gospel to consider the great speeches and the passion of Jesus in more detail than other events in the story.

Causation in Matthew

When the principle of causation is applied to Matthew, the events of the passion narrative become significant in a way that the great

45

speeches do not. Numerous statements in Matthew's Gospel establish causal links between events, and a great many of these ultimately link events to Jesus' death on the cross. We have already seen how Jesus' seeming disregard for Sabbath laws and his claim to be "lord of the Sabbath" cause the religious leaders to plot his murder (12:1-14). Similarly, his teaching causes people to take offense at him (13:53-57) and his mighty works lead to accusations that he is demonic (9:34; 12:24). At other times, Jesus' words and deeds cause people to be impressed by his authority (7:28-29; 9:8, 33), but this too is connected to the Passion insofar as we are told the religious leaders deliver him to Pilate "out of envy" (27:18). Bauer has suggested that the entire section of Matthew that deals with Jesus' ministry to Israel (4:17—16:20) is related to that section which deals with his passion and resurrection (16:21—28:20) through the principle of causation.[23] Matthew tells the story of Jesus' ministry of teaching, preaching, and healing in a way that explains why Israel rejected and crucified its Messiah.

The passion narrative, then, is not simply an epilogue attached to the end of Matthew's Gospel, but is the goal of the entire narrative. Matthew's reader comes to realize that this is in fact the purpose of Jesus' life and ministry: he has come to give his life as a ransom for many (20:28). This affirmation recalls the angel's proleptic announcement at the narrative's beginning that Jesus would "save his people from their sin" (1:21).[24] This, then, is what the story is about. The great speeches of Jesus, on the other hand, must be viewed as serving some subsidiary purpose in the narrative, for they do not define the overall development of the story. The speeches certainly represent a slowing of discourse time that directs the reader to consider the material as possessing special significance. At the same time, however, the reader of Matthew's story realizes that Jesus has not come to give speeches but to give his life. He has come to save people from their sin and he will accomplish this not through the speeches but through the blood of the covenant, which is "poured out for many for the forgiveness of sins" (26:28). The events of the passion narrative present a great consummation of purpose toward which the other events in the story are directed.

Conflict Analysis in Matthew

These observations are confirmed when we turn to an analysis of conflict in Matthew. On the surface, conflict appears to develop primarily along two lines: between Jesus and the religious leaders and between Jesus and his own disciples. The conflict with the religious leaders is defined in terms of their opposition to Jesus as one who claims to have divine authority. As this conflict develops in the story, the religious leaders test Jesus (16:1; 19:3; 22:18, 34), challenge him (21:15, 23), make accusations against him (9:3, 34; 12:24), try to "entangle him in his talk" (22:15), and even plot to kill him (12:14; 26:3-4). The reader realizes that the worst that could happen with regard to this conflict would be for the leaders' plot against Jesus to succeed. This, of course, is precisely what does happen when the conflict is resolved in Matthew's passion narrative.

The conflict between Jesus and his own disciples is defined in terms of their opposition to Jesus as one who insists upon suffering and servanthood as constitutive of discipleship. Within the story, they demonstrate a failure to grasp this essential component of his teaching (see, for example, 19:13-14, 23-25; 20:20-28) and even rebuke him for thinking this way (16:22). The worst that could happen with regard to this conflict, the reader imagines, would be for the disciples to reject Jesus altogether and cease to follow him. Once again, this is exactly what does happen when the conflict is resolved in Matthew's passion narrative (26:56, 69-75).

Because it is difficult to believe that Matthew would resolve these conflicts so negatively, some might suggest that the real resolution does not come until the resurrection of Jesus and the giving of the great commission in chapter 28. Thus, the religious leaders only appear to succeed in their plot to kill Jesus; they actually fail because Jesus does not stay dead. Similarly, Jesus' disciples appear to desert him, but we later learn that they come back and are sent out on a new mission to all nations. The problem with this view is that it trivializes the very real losses suffered by Jesus in the passion narrative. Matthew does not set the reader up with an extended account of false resolutions in the passion story only to overturn these with a few brief verses at the Gospel's end.

A better understanding is gained through the realization that neither Jesus' conflict with the religious leaders nor his conflict with his disciples is ultimately definitive of the Gospel's plot. What this narrative is really about is conflict on a deeper level, namely, conflict between God and Satan. Of course, the conflict is not presented as God versus Satan *per se*, for that would be no contest. Rather, it is "God at work in Jesus" who is opposed to Satan (cf. 13:36-43). As the supreme agent of God, Jesus comes to save God's people from their sin by giving his

47

life as a ransom for many and by shedding his blood to establish a new covenant of forgiveness. Satan challenges Jesus specifically as God's Son (4:1-11) and, indirectly, remains active throughout the story. Satan is identified as the force behind the disciples' resistance to Jesus (16:23). Likewise, the religious leaders behave in a manner reminiscent of Satan when they "test" Jesus. The great irony of Matthew's Gospel, however, is that whereas the religious leaders want to bring Jesus to the cross, Satan wants to keep him from it (cf. 16:21-23). Accordingly, the conflict between Jesus (or God) and Satan is also resolved in Matthew's passion narrative, but this conflict is clearly resolved in Jesus' favor. When Jesus dies on the cross, he fulfills the will of God (cf. 26:39, 42) and defeats the will of Satan. Ironically, Jesus must "lose" his conflicts with the religious leaders and with his own disciples in order to win the greater conflict with Satan. The story of the resurrection and the great commission does not cancel out these losses, but renews the relationships in light of what has transpired. The religious leaders, we learn, continue to oppose Jesus (28:11-15) and the disciples continue to doubt (28:17). Nevertheless, Jesus has saved God's people from their sin and so can initiate a new mission, one that is based on his universal authority and abiding presence.[25]

Conclusions Regarding Matthew's Plot

The plot of Matthew's Gospel is basically the story of its central character, Jesus. The fact that this seems obvious today is a sign of how far biblical scholarship has come in developing an appreciation for the narrative quality of the Gospels. Earlier in this century, Matthew was read as a catechism, as a lectionary, or as an administrative manual, but theories that it was a story about Jesus were controversial.[26]

This story about Jesus, however, is set within the broader perspective of a story about God. Matthew's temporal perspective is not limited to the events of Jesus' life but extends from creation to the close of the age. It is God's point of view that Matthew establishes as normative for his story. In fact, the most significant thing about Jesus in Matthew's narrative is that he is the Son of God and, as such, comes to save God's people from their sin.

The plot of Matthew's Gospel is episodic, but the episodes that comprise it are not unrelated. Numerous episodes serve to develop the conflict between Jesus and the religious leaders and to explain how it happens that Israel rejects Jesus and puts him to death. A separate set of episodes develop conflict between Jesus and his disciples and serve to explain why they ultimately desert him.

More than one line of development, then, can be discerned in the plot of Matthew's Gospel. Ultimately, it may be best to speak of a main plot and various subplots rather than attempting to describe the narrative in terms of a single chain of events.[27] One may speak meaningfully of plot developments concerning the overarching conflict between God and Satan as well as concerning the more obvious conflicts between Jesus and the religious leaders or between Jesus and his own disciples. It is significant, therefore, that all of these plot lines find their resolution in the events surrounding Jesus' arrest and crucifixion.

As I understand it, the main plot of Matthew's Gospel concerns the divine plan by which God's rule will be established and God's people will be saved from sin. This plan is introduced in the first part of the Gospel, where Jesus is presented as the Son of God, the one through whom God is "with us" (1:23). God is pleased with Jesus (3:17) and, through Jesus, intends to save people from sin (1:21). The reader soon learns, however, that Satan challenges Jesus as the Son of God and intends to thwart God's purpose (4:1-11).

In the second part of Matthew's Gospel, the focus shifts from a direct presentation of conflict between God and Satan to a development of conflict between human characters, especially Jesus and the religious leaders. In a sense, however, this is but a representation of the greater struggle that continues beneath the surface. The religious leaders, like Satan, are evil (9:4; 12:34, 39, 45; 16:4; cf. 13:19, 38). They test Jesus and challenge his divine authority. As he goes about his mission of teaching, preaching, and healing, they seem determined to thwart his efforts to bring salvation to God's people. In fact, they are quite successful at this and it becomes clear that Israel will reject Jesus and the salvation he offers.

With Jesus' first passion prediction (16:21-23), however, the main plot of Matthew's Gospel receives a new twist. This prolepsis reveals that, ironically, the religious leaders' rejection and eventual crucifixion of Jesus is in keeping with God's plan and is, in fact, the very thing Satan would prevent. Subsequent prolepses reveal that it is through Jesus' death that God's people will be saved from their sin (20:28). The passion narrative, then, is told with tremendous irony, for here it is related that the religious leaders prevail in their superficial conflict with Jesus, but by so doing unwittingly fulfill the plan of God and resolve the deeper conflict with Satan in Jesus' favor.

Matthew's Gospel is more complex than this sketch suggests. Intertwined is the subplot involving Jesus and his disciples, the characters with whom the implied reader may identify most closely. Matthew 28 also gives some added perspective to the apparent defeats Jesus suffers by briefly showing both the religious leaders and Jesus' disciples in a post-resurrection light.[28] In addition, the great speeches of Jesus presented at various points in the Gospel address the implied reader with a special immediacy that is enhanced on repeated readings.[29] Still, this analysis should be sufficient to demonstrate that Matthew's Gospel does have a plot and that light can be shed on the interpretation of this plot through the application of established criteria for narrative criticism.[30]

5

Characters

Although the last chapter dealt ostensibly with events, it also had a good bit to say about characters. This is because, to adapt a metaphor from Perrine, characters and events are like two riders on a seesaw: movement at either end affects the other and it is the interaction of both that makes the plot work.[1] As novelist Henry James put it, "What is character but the determination of incident? What is incident but the illustration of character?"[2]

Characters are the actors in a story, the ones who carry out the various activities that comprise the plot. We think of them as people, though of course in some literature they may be animals, robots, or other nonhuman entities. A serpent plays a major role in the third chapter of Genesis and, in Judges 9:8-15, even the trees function as characters. Angels and demons make various appearances as nonhuman characters in the Gospels.

We should not limit our conception of characters to individuals, since it is possible for a group to function as a single character. In our Gospels, this is true not only of the crowds that follow Jesus but also of his disciples and the religious leaders. When the narrative reports that the disciples do something or say something, the reader does not imagine that these 12 individuals actually move or speak in unison. Such stereotyping is a conventional literary device by which a number of characters are made to serve a single role.

A NARRATIVE UNDERSTANDING OF CHARACTERS

Characters are constructs of the implied author, created to fulfill a particular role in the story. They are best regarded, however, as open

51

constructs,[3] whose existence sometimes transcends the purpose for which they are created. Vivid characters, such as Sherlock Holmes or Ebeneezer Scrooge, seem to take on a life of their own, apart from the stories about them. The implied reader may find it easy to imagine what they would say or do in circumstances not reported in the stories. Yet such speculation is not without bounds; it is based on evidence about the characters drawn from the narratives. Thus, narrative critics are interested in characterization, that is, the process through which the implied author provides the implied reader with what is necessary to reconstruct a character from the narrative.

Telling and Showing

Booth makes a simple yet profound observation: The implied author can reveal characters either by telling the reader about them or by showing the reader what the characters are like within the story itself.[4]

The technique of *telling* employs the voice of a reliable narrator to speak directly to the reader. Homer, for instance, tells the reader outright that Odysseus is "heroic," "admirable," and "wise." In modern literature, the technique of telling is often considered stilted, intrusive, or pedantic. But in our Gospels the method thrives: Matthew tells us that Joseph is a "just" man (1:19) and that John is "the one spoken of by the prophet" (3:3). Luke informs us that Zechariah and Elizabeth are "righteous before God" and "blameless" (1:6). Statements such as these present the implied author's view of the characters in a way that is blatant but accessible.

Even in the Gospels, however, the preferred method of characterization seems to be the technique of *showing*. An implied author can show the reader what characters are like through statements that present either their own point of view or the point of view of other characters concerning them. Boris Uspensky's studies on point of view suggest that such characterization takes place on four planes: the *spatial temporal* plane refers to actions, the *phraseological* plane to speech, the *psychological* plane to thoughts, and the *ideological* plane to belief and values.[5]

The technique of showing is less precise than that of telling but it is usually more interesting. The reader must work harder, collecting data from various sources and evaluating it in order to figure out the implied author's view of the characters. One must consider the reliability of the character whose point of view is presented. When John the Baptist calls the religious leaders a "brood of vipers" (Matt. 3:7), does the implied author intend for the reader also to regard them as a brood of vipers? Since John has been directly characterized as the one "spoken of by the prophet" (3:3), it is likely that his point of view is reliable. Later in the story, when Jesus (who has proved to be a completely reliable character) declares that John himself is a prophet and, in fact, "more than a prophet" (11:9), his credibility seems assured. If any doubt remains as to the accuracy of his assessment of the religious leaders, it is shortly removed when Jesus also refers to them as "a brood of vipers" (12:34; cf. 23:34).

At times, however, the reader must dismiss such characterizations as unreliable. When the religious leaders characterize Jesus as one who "casts out demons by the prince of demons" (Matt. 9:34), the reader realizes that this is incorrect, and in fact reveals more about the religious leaders themselves than it does about Jesus (cf. Matt. 12:22-37).

The technique of showing also compels the reader to compare and evaluate different kinds of evidence. Herod is characterized on the phraseological plane as one who wants to worship Jesus (Matt. 2:8) but on the spatial-temporal plane as one who wants to kill him (Matt. 2:16). By presenting the reader with such a dilemma early in his narrative, Matthew rather subtly introduces an important theme of his Gospel: deeds are more revealing than talk (cf. 7:21; 23:2-3).

The implied authors of our Gospels, then, use techniques of both telling and showing to reveal the characters in their narratives. But what is revealed? Two aspects of characterization are especially important: evaluative point of view and character traits.

Evaluative Point of View

We have already spoken, in chapter 3, of evaluative point of view as the general perspective that an implied author establishes as normative for a work. We can also speak of the evaluative point of view of any given character or character group within the story. In this sense, the term refers to the norms, values, and general worldview that govern the way a character looks at things and renders judgments upon them.[6] Strictly speaking, any statement on the ideological plane may give a character's evaluative point of view concerning one thing or another. For example, the statement about the Sadducees in Mark 12:18 gives their evaluative point of view concerning the doctrine of resurrection. In practice, however, the term is usually used to describe the general orientation of a character toward truth or untruth. This orientation may be revealed through narration on any of the four planes.

In all of our Gospels, there are only two basic points of view, the "true" and the "untrue," and the evaluative points of view of all characters may be defined accordingly.[7] Unlike some modern authors, our Gospel writers do not allow characters to hover ambiguously between these two poles. Since the narrators of our Gospels are reliable, their evaluative points of view are always true. In addition, the evaluative point of view of God is by definition true and that of Satan untrue.

What about the other characters? The reader will judge whether their evaluative points of view are true by comparing them with the points of view of the narrator, God, and Satan. In Mark's Gospel, Jesus is seen to espouse a true evaluative point of view because he always acts, speaks, thinks, and believes in ways that accord with God's point of view. The religious leaders, on the other hand, espouse a point of view inconsistent with that of God. They misinterpret Scripture in ways that "make void the word of God" (7:13) and, whereas God is pleased to call Jesus "Son" (1:11), the religious leaders find such an identification appalling (14:61-64). The disciples of Jesus in Mark's Gospel switch their allegiance back and forth; at times they appear to espouse God's viewpoint while at other times (notably 8:33) they do not.

Character Traits

Characters may also be distinguished by traits that are attributed to them in the narrative. Chatman describes characters as "paradigms of traits" and quotes psychologist J. P. Guilford's definition of a trait as "any distinguishable, relatively enduring way in which one individual differs from another."[8] For narrative purposes, traits are considered to be persistent personal qualities that describe the character involved: Ebeneezer Scrooge is "stingy," and Sherlock Holmes is "perceptive."

Sometimes the adjectives that define a character's traits are found explicitly in the text. The narrator of Luke's Gospel, for example, tells us that Zechariah and Elizabeth are "righteous" and "blameless" (1:6). But since characterization is often more a process of showing than telling, traits sometimes must be inferred. Such inference does not involve "psychologizing" of characters on the basis of insights extraneous to the text, but rather calls for recognizing assumptions that the text makes of its implied reader. In Luke 16:14, the reader is explicitly told that the religious leaders are "lovers of money," but in the immediately preceding verse the reader has heard Jesus say that anyone

54

who tries to serve both God and mammon will "love the one and hate the other." Accordingly, the trait that is explicitly ascribed to the religious leaders in 16:14 ("money-loving") implies another trait ("God-hating").[9]

Narrative critics sometimes distinguish different kinds of characters on the basis of their traits. The best-known such distinction is that which Forster makes between *round characters,* who possess a variety of potentially conflicting traits, and *flat characters,* whose traits are all consistent and predictable.[10] Abrams has further proposed the designation of *stock characters* for those with a single trait who perform a perfunctory role in the story.[11]

In Luke's Gospel, the widow that Jesus praises in 21:1-4 is a stock character. Her only role in the story is to illustrate what it means to be "sacrificial." Most of the religious leaders should probably be classed as flat characters, for the traits ascribed to them ("unloving," "hypocritical," "self-righteous," and so on) fall into a consistent pattern. Jesus' disciples, on the other hand, are the best example of round characters in Luke. They can be "humble" (5:8), "self-denying" (5:11), and "loyal" (22:28), but they can also be "arrogant" (22:33), "status-conscious" (22:24), and "cowardly" (22:54-62).

Jesus is consistently portrayed in a positive light, but the traits ascribed to him are varied and at times surprising. He is both "censorious" (11:37-52) and "conciliatory" (23:34) with regard to his enemies. He can be either "receptive" (9:11) or "precautionary" (9:57-62; 14:25-33) toward those who wish to follow him. He is "elated" over those who have received God's revelation (10:21-22) but "grieved" for those who have not (19:41-44). Thus Jesus, like the disciples, is a round character. The difference is that Jesus, despite his range of diverse character traits, consistently espouses the evaluative point of view of God. The disciples are not only inconsistent in the traits that they evince but also in their allegiance to God's point of view.

Some literary theorists also like to speak of characters as *static* or *dynamic,* depending on whether their basic profile changes over the course of the narrative. In accord with such a typology, Jesus would be viewed as a static character in Luke's Gospel since, even though he grows physically and "increases in wisdom" (2:40, 52), his character traits and evaluative point of view remain the same. The disciples in Luke (and especially in Luke-Acts!) are more dynamic.

Empathy, Sympathy, and Antipathy

Literature inspires the imagination. We probably all have had the experience of reading ourselves into a story at times, of imagining in the course of reading that we are there somewhere among the characters of the story world. Literary critics call such an effect *empathy*. It has been described variously as an "involuntary projection," as an "inner mimicry," and as an observer's participation in the sensation of that which is perceived.[12]

How is such an effect achieved? Readers are most likely to empathize with characters who are similar to them (*realistic empathy*) or with characters who represent what they would like to be (*idealistic empathy*). In literary terms, empathy between the implied reader and any given character must be established on the basis of common evaluative point of view and character traits.

Since the implied reader of Matthew favors the evaluative point of view of God, possibility for empathy exists with either Jesus or his disciples. Identification with Jesus will be idealistic, in that he represents the perfect model for what the implied reader would like to be. To some extent, such identification is encouraged by statements in Matthew that affirm the continuing presence of Jesus beyond the bounds of the story itself (cf. 18:15-20; 25:31-45; 28:20). The implied reader is encouraged to imagine that he or she is part of a community in which Jesus is still present and through which Jesus still speaks and acts. In other respects, however, empathy with Jesus is severely limited in Matthew's narrative. Although the implied reader and Jesus share a commitment to God's evaluative point of view, the character of Jesus is defined by a number of traits that the implied reader could never own. Jesus is "saving" (1:21), "authoritative" (23:8, 10), and, for that matter, "eternally present" (18:20; 28:20) in ways to which the implied reader would never aspire. Accordingly, the implied reader's tendency to empathize with the character of Jesus in Matthew's story will be cut short by Jesus' own warnings against those who would say, "I am the Christ" (24:5).

The best possibility for realistic empathy in Matthew's Gospel is offered by Jesus' disciples. Not only do they usually favor God's point of view, but they also are characterized by traits likely to be shared by the reader. In Matthew, the disciples are persons of "little faith" (6:30; 8:26; 14:31; 16:8), persons whose spirits are willing, though their flesh is weak (26:41). They grow in understanding, but they do not always get the point right away (16:5-12). Their experience includes failure (26:56), but also renewed commitment (28:16-20). In fact, the disciples in Matthew's story are sometimes anachronistically referred to as "the church," that is, as the community outside Matthew's story world to which the implied reader certainly belongs (18:17; cf. 16:18). In one place, Matthew's narrator even interrupts an address of Jesus to his disciples in order to speak directly to the reader (24:15). Such a practice assumes that Matthew's reader is empathizing with the disciples at this point and applying Jesus' words to his or her own situation.

The literary concept of *sympathy* is related to that of empathy, but assumes a less intense identification. Instead of a "feeling-into" a character, sympathy consists of a "feeling-alongside-of."[13] The implied reader may feel sympathy for characters even if they do not share his or her evaluative point of view. Like empathy, sympathy is viewed by narrative critics as a literary effect created by the implied author. One of the simplest means of arousing the reader's sympathy for a character is to attribute such sympathy to another character with whom the reader has come to empathize. As a general rule, the reader of a narrative will care the most about those characters for whom the protagonist cares the most. This is because the protagonist is usually one character with whom the reader experiences some degree of empathy.

That the disciples of Jesus are portrayed more harshly in the Gospel of Mark than they are in Matthew is well known. Although the reader may at times empathize with the disciples in Mark (13:14), such an identification will be more limited here. Still, Mark's reader cares about the disciples in a way that he or she does not care about Jesus' opponents in this story. Why? Because Jesus himself, as the protagonist in the story, cares about them. The reader empathizes with Jesus' desire for them to succeed as well as with his confidence that they ultimately will (13:9-13).

Antipathy, feelings of alienation from or disdain for particular characters, is created in the same way as positive sympathetic responses. If the implied reader empathizes with a character who feels aversion toward other characters, then the implied reader also will feel aversion toward those characters.

Empathy, sympathy, and antipathy relate to identifications made by the reader with characters in a narrative. Readers are sometimes also led by stories to make such identifications with real people in the real world. Harriett Beecher Stowe's novel *Uncle Tom's Cabin* aroused the sympathy of readers not only for the characters in the story but also for African-American people in general. Matthew's Gospel, on the other hand, has sometimes aroused antipathy toward Jewish people and even provoked hostility against them. In either case, narrative critics would regard such considerations as extraneous to the task of interpreting a text *as literature*. They seek to avoid the *referential fallacy* of interpreting literary elements in terms of supposed antecedents in the real world.

CASE STUDY: THE RELIGIOUS LEADERS IN THE SYNOPTIC GOSPELS

Scholars are widely agreed that the religious leaders constitute a character group in Matthew, in Mark, and in Luke, and so can be treated as a single character in each of these stories. Included in this character group are such subgroups as Pharisees, Sadducees, chief priests, elders, scribes, and lawyers. Although distinctions between these subgroups are sometimes noted, the Gospel narratives also tend to lump them together through such combined references as "Pharisees and Sadducees" or "chief priests, scribes, and elders."[14] While it may be possible to speak precisely of the characterization of any particular subgroup of religious leaders in these Gospels, it is also possible to speak more broadly of the characterization of religious leaders in general.[15]

Telling and Showing: Characterization of Religious Leaders

In the synoptic Gospels, the technique of telling is used very sparingly. In Matthew and Mark, it is used only once with regard to the religious leaders, when we are told that they (unlike Jesus) do not have authority (Matt. 7:29; Mark 1:22). In Luke, it is used slightly more often, though notably not to convey the information about authority found in Matthew and Mark. Instead, we are told that the religious leaders are "lovers of money" (16:14), that they "reject the purpose of God for themselves" (7:30), and that they "trust in themselves that they are righteous and despise others" (18:9).[16]

The method of showing is used to characterize the religious leaders on all four planes of expression (spatial-temporal, phraseological, psychological, and ideological). Reports of their actions, thoughts, and beliefs serve as reliable indicators of who they are and what they are about. Reports of their speech are also significant, but in a manner deserving further comment. Descriptions of the leaders offered through

58

the speech of other characters are generally accurate. The leaders' own phraseology, however, does not usually provide an accurate portrait of them unless they speak about a character to someone else. When they address the character who is the subject of their speech, their phraseology almost never reveals what they are really like. A few examples from Matthew will illustrate this.[17]

The religious leaders make the following statements directly to Jesus himself:

"Teacher, we wish to see a sign from you" (12:38);

"Is it lawful to divorce one's wife for any cause?" (19:3);

"Teacher, we know that you are true and teach the way of God truthfully" (22:16).

Yet they make the following statements about Jesus to others:

"This man is blaspheming" (9:3);

"He casts out demons by the prince of demons" (9:34);

"He deserves death" (26:66).

Only the indirect phraseology of the leaders accurately conveys the opposition between them and Jesus. The first three statements also occur in contexts of intense conflict, but this is not expressed in their speech. In these instances, Matthew overrides the image of the leaders as presented through their own phraseology by offering a contradictory image on some other plane. In some cases he informs the reader, on the psychological plane, that the leaders seek to "test" Jesus (19:3) or to "entangle him in his talk" (22:15). At other times, the more reliable phraseology of Jesus reveals the opposition that is not apparent in the leaders' own words: he responds insightfully to their seemingly innocuous remarks with harsh words of condemnation, denouncing them for things their speech did not reveal (12:39-42; 22:18).

This pattern of speech is typical of the religious leaders in each of the synoptic Gospels. As a result, the leaders often seem polite to Jesus, but he is not at all courteous to them. The implied reader, however, does not conclude that the leaders are polite, but rather that they are devious and hypocritical. They criticize the disciples to Jesus and Jesus to his disciples, but almost never attack people "to their face."[18] Accordingly, Jesus is often placed in the position of responding to their thoughts or to what they have said about him to others. In Jesus' own speech, by contrast, no such distinction can be made; there is no difference between what he says directly to the religious leaders and what he says about them to others.

Evaluative Point of View of the Religious Leaders

In each of the synoptic Gospels, the religious leaders are presented as characters who espouse a point of view opposed to that of God. The manner in which this is construed, however, differs somewhat in the three books.

In Mark, the leaders are frequently in error because, as Jesus tells one group, they know "neither the scriptures nor the power of God" (12:24). Their ignorance of Scripture actually consists of misinterpretations that result from reading Scripture according to a human point of view. They think, for instance, that they have found justification for ignoring the command to honor one's parents (7:9-13) and for legitimizing divorce (10:4-9). Jesus, who is able to interpret Scripture in accord with God's evaluative point of view, denounces such interpretations and accuses them of forsaking God's commandments in favor of what is only human tradition (7:8). Two divergent views emerge in Mark, then, as to what it means to do the will of God. Jesus correctly identifies the doing of God's will with exercising love (12:28-31) but the leaders repeatedly define it in terms of their own legalistic prescriptions (2:24; 3:2; 7:1-5). Ironically, they fail to realize the extent to which the Scriptures they cite actually prophesy against them (7:6-7).

If the religious leaders do not understand Scripture, neither do they understand the power of God. They mistakenly attribute Jesus' mighty works to the power of Beelzebul and regard Jesus as one who is demon-possessed (3:22). God is pleased to call Jesus "Son," but the leaders regard such thinking as blasphemous (14:61-64; cf. 2:7).

It is not simply that the leaders in Mark are wrong about Scripture, wrong about Jesus, and wrong about so many other things. The very bases on which they make such judgments are wrong: their norms and standards for making decisions derive from human authority. They fear what people think of them (11:32; 12:12; cf. 10:28) and value superficial displays of honor (12:38-40). The only exception to this consistent portrayal is the wise scribe who, near the end of the story, concurs with Jesus' teaching and so recognizes the superiority of God's viewpoint over that of the scribe's colleagues (12:28-34).

Much of what we have observed in Mark's Gospel would be true for Matthew and Luke as well. These two narratives, however, go beyond Mark in explicating why the leaders hold to such a false perspective.

In Matthew, the religious leaders hold to a human point of view because they are incapable of receiving revelation from God. Early in

60

the narrative the reader notices that, whereas the Magi are granted divine revelation to keep them from inadvertently assisting Herod, the religious leaders receive no such assistance (2:1-12). Later, Jesus performs a work of healing that should reveal the true nature and source of his authority to them, but unlike the crowds who also witness the miracle, they do not respond with any new insight (9:6-8). Incredibly, even news of Jesus' resurrection (the "sign of Jonah," 12:40) fails to have any effect on them (28:11-15). This characterization is in keeping with a theme developed throughout Matthew, namely, that "understanding" is something that must be given by God.[19] The religious leaders do not understand because understanding is not given to them (cf. 11:25-27). As such, their false point of view is more deeply entrenched here than in Mark. There is no wise scribe in Matthew who is capable of recognizing the truth when confronted with it. Rather, one of Matthew's favorite words for the religious leaders is "blind": they are incapable of seeing the truth even when it is right in front of them (15:14; 23:16, 17, 19, 24, 26).

In Luke's story, the leaders are not blind, but "foolish" (11:40). They possess the key of knowledge but will not use it (11:52). Whereas in Matthew the religious leaders are rejected by John as ineligible for baptism (3:7), in Luke it is the leaders who reject "God's purpose for themselves" by not accepting John's baptism (7:30). The theme of "the rebuffed invitation" runs throughout Luke's story in a manner illustrative of the religious leaders' point of view. Although the leaders may claim to look forward to celebrating God's rule (14:15), in reality they have declined invitations to do so (14:16-24). Like the older brother in the prodigal son parable, they "refuse to go in" because the celebration is not given in their honor (15:25-29). Because the leaders have so foolishly rejected the things of God, they may be characterized as people who "do not know what they are doing" (23:34). Yet this lack of true knowledge is not presented as a judgment of God upon them; rather, it is construed as a possible excuse, on the basis of which they should be forgiven.

Character Traits of the Religious Leaders

The character traits ascribed to the religious leaders in each of the synoptic Gospels are in keeping with the foregoing analysis of their evaluative point of view. The leaders are flat characters, but the dominant characteristic attributed to them is different in each work.

In Mark's story, the root character trait of the religious leaders is that they are "without authority" (1:22).[20] This is the first thing that the reader learns about them[21] and it is the only trait considered so important that the implied author has the narrator tell the reader this outright. To be without authority means, of course, to be without divine authority. The leaders in Mark, as we have seen, have only a human understanding of Scripture, and so they are frequently "in error." This lack of understanding, in turn, causes them to be "accusatory" with regard to both Jesus and his disciples, unjustifiably criticizing them when no wrong has been done (2:15-27). The irony in Mark's portrayal, however, is that religious *leaders* are shown to be without authority. Thus, they are remiss *as leaders*, leaving the people to become "as sheep without a shepherd" (6:34). They are, in fact, "fearful" of the people (11:18; 12:12; 14:1-2) and are only able to maintain their position by being "manipulative" (15:9-13) and "hypocritical" (12:38-40). Similarly, in their dealings with Jesus they are "conspiratorial" (15:1), and "deceitful" (14:1), traits that would be unnecessary if they possessed any true authority. Eventually it is revealed that a primary reason for the leaders' opposition to Jesus is that they are "envious" of him (15:10), since he possesses the authority they lack (1:22).

In Matthew's story, the leaders are also without authority (7:28-29) and all of the traits just associated with them in Mark are ascribed to them here as well. Matthew, however, establishes another quality, more basic than a simple lack of authority, as the root character trait for the religious leaders in his narrative. That quality, as indicated by Kingsbury, is "evil."[22] The leaders are never called evil in Mark (or in Luke[23]), but they are explicitly identified as such several times in Matthew (9:4; 12:34, 39, 45; 16:4; 22:18). In addition, reliable characters in Matthew's story, such as Jesus and John the Baptist, describe them with such epithets as "brood of vipers" (3:7; 12:34; 23:32) and "child of hell" (23:15), which clearly depict them as evil.

What does it mean in Matthew's story world to be "evil"? Ultimately, it implies an implacable opposition to God and a fundamental association with Satan, who is "the evil one" (13:19, 38). According to a parable found only in Matthew, the world (that is, the world of Matthew's story) may be likened to a field in which wheat and tares grow side by side (13:24-30). The tares represent people who were not placed in the world by God, but who were sown by an enemy, the devil. They serve no useful purpose and their destiny is the fire. Matthew presents the religious leaders in exactly this light (15:13). As

62

evil characters, they are aligned with Satan and stand under condemnation.

The root character trait for the religious leaders in Luke's story is not evil but "self-righteousness." Of course, the leaders have many faults, but in this regard they are not so different from many other characters with whom Jesus interacts. Their problem is not that they are especially *un*righteous, but that they are *self*-righteous; they are not aware of their need for repentance. The narrator of Luke's story refers to them as people who "pretend to be righteous" (20:20) and describes one of them as a person who seeks to "make himself righteous" (10:29). Jesus also describes the leaders as persons who "make themselves righteous before humans" (16:15) and he tells a parable in which one of them proclaims his own righteousness (18:10-12). At other points, Jesus uses parabolic speech to confront them with their own point of view; they see themselves as characters who are "righteous" (5:32) and "well" (5:31), who need little forgiveness (7:41), who do not need to repent (15:7), and who can claim life-long service and obedience to God (15:29).

As the root character trait of the leaders in Luke's story, self-righteousness accounts for other traits that they exhibit. Because the leaders are self-righteous, they also prove to be "unloving." At one point, Jesus explains to Simon the Pharisee that only those who have experienced much forgiveness are capable of showing much love (7:40-47). The religious leaders in Luke's story lack love for God (11:42; cf. 16:13-14) and love for neighbor (10:31-32). They continually look down on other people, such as the tax collectors and sinners with whom Jesus associates (5:31-32; 15:1-2), because they do not realize that they are sinners themselves. They are people who "trust in themselves that they are righteous and despise others" (18:9).

The root character trait ascribed to the religious leaders in each of the Gospel narratives accords with the presentation of their evaluative point of view in that story. In Mark, the religious leaders evaluate everything according to human standards and, as a result, they may be paradoxically characterized as leaders who have no real authority. In Matthew, because the leaders are evil they are incapable of receiving revelation from God. They are blind because they are evil, not vice versa. In Luke, the leaders are self-righteous, and this explains why they refuse to accept the invitations that are offered to them. Their satisfaction with being righteous in the eyes of people prevents them from accepting God's viewpoint and being made righteous before God (18:14).

Empathy, Sympathy, and Antipathy Regarding the Religious Leaders

The implied reader does not empathize with the religious leaders in any of these three Gospels, because in all three they are portrayed as espousing a false evaluative point of view. But will the reader regard them with sympathy or antipathy?

With Mark's Gospel, the situation is somewhat ambiguous since Jesus' feelings for them surface only occasionally. Once, he is said to be angry at them, grieved at their "hardness of heart" (3:5). Another time, they cause him to "sigh deeply in his spirit," that is, to feel exasperation. These brief negative expressions are not enough to provoke antipathy, however, for Jesus expresses some of the same feelings for his own disciples (e.g., 8:17-21) and yet he obviously cares for them. What is different about Jesus' attitude toward the religious leaders is that he regards them as characters who will ultimately be condemned in the judgment (12:9, 40; 14:62). The implied reader regards such impending judgment as "the Lord's doing" and as "marvelous" (12:10). This delight in the eventual downfall of the leaders assumes complete lack of sympathy for them and their cause. Still, this is mitigated by the fact that Mark also introduces a few "exceptions" into his narrative, characters such as the wise scribe who is "not far from the Kingdom of God" (12:34) and Joseph of Arimathea, "a respected member of the council who was also looking for the kingdom of God" (15:43). These characters indicate that it might be possible for individual religious leaders to escape the judgment that is promised to come upon the group as a whole. Thus, the reader of Mark's story feels some antipathy toward the religious leaders as a character group, but some sympathy for individual characters who may be distinguished from the group as a whole.

In Matthew's story, antipathy for the leaders is the rule. There are no exceptions in his story—no wise scribe, no ruler of the synagogue whom Jesus helps, no member of the council who comes to bury Jesus. Matthew's characterization of the leaders is consistent: they are evil, they are aligned with Satan, and everything they do, say, think, and believe is wrong.[24] Jesus' attitude toward them is likewise consistent. He does not attempt to minister to them any more than he would to the demons he exorcises. He does not try to teach them the truth because he knows they are incapable of receiving revelation from God. They are "blind guides" and, as such, should be simply left alone (15:14). He does not even call them to repentance, but rather regards them as completely ineligible for admission to the kingdom of heaven from the very start (5:20). They are, in fact, a plant that God did not plant, destined to be rooted up (15:13; cf. 13:24-30, 36-43). The kingdom of God will be taken away from them and given to others (21:43). Jesus, with whom the implied reader idealistically empathizes, shows absolutely no concern or sympathy for any of the religious leaders, individually or as a group. Accordingly, the implied reader feels no sympathy for them either. Rather, the implied reader is gratified to learn that God will ultimately triumph over these evil characters, that Jesus himself will be their judge (26:64) and that all of them, without exception, will be "put to a miserable death" (21:41) and "sentenced to hell" (23:33).

Luke's story is different. Here, the religious leaders are not evil but self-righteous, not blind but foolish. The difference between these formulations is significant. Within the story world of Matthew's Gospel, "evil" and "blind" represent unchangeable qualities that are intrinsic to the religious leaders' characterization. But in Luke, Jesus tells them the benefits they will receive if they change their ways: "Do this, and you will live" (10:28); "everything will be clean for you" (11:41); "you will be repaid at the resurrection" (14:14). No statements like these are ever found in Matthew, where the judgment against them has already been made and their ultimate condemnation is assured. In Luke, the invitation remains open. Like the older brother in the story of the prodigal son, the leaders may yet decide to put aside their folly and accept the way of God. Still, it is significant that within Luke's Gospel, not a single religious leader ever makes this change.[25]

With regard to the religious leaders, then, Luke's story is a tragedy,[26] a tale of unfulfilled hope and unrealized possibility. Their conflict with Jesus, furthermore, is somewhat one-sided; they reject his invitations but he does not reject theirs. He eats with them (7:36; 11:37; 14:1) and includes them in his ministry of teaching (10:25-37; 11:37-41; 14:12-14; 15:1-32; 17:20-21) and healing (8:40-42, 49-56; 22:15-19). If he warns them of the dire consequences of their predicament (11:50-51; 20:15-19), he also weeps over their failure to accept the salvation he brings (19:41-44) and pleads for them to be forgiven all the same (23:34). In short, he expresses sympathy for them, not hostility, and thus the implied reader will surely regard them with sympathy also.

65

Conclusions on Characterization of Religious Leaders

Traditional interpretations of the synoptic Gospels have evaluated their portrayal of the religious leaders in terms of historical accuracy. It has often been suggested that these depictions are unreliable, having been tainted by the polemics and rivalry that existed between Jewish and Christian groups in the first century. Narrative criticism offers an alternative approach. Characterization of the leaders in each of the Gospel stories is not evaluated in terms of historical reference, but in terms of the contribution made to the overall literary effect of the work.

In the Gospel of Mark, the leaders serve as "foils" for illustrating dramatically what it means to think the things of people instead of the things of God. This is particularly true with regard to the issue of authority, which in Mark is clearly the crux of their conflict with Jesus.[27] The leaders exemplify what human authority is like: oppressive, presumptuous, and self-seeking. In stark contrast to this, Jesus demonstrates what authority that pleases God is like: true authority shows itself in humble service and is willing to accept suffering and to make sacrifices for the sake of others (10:45). The great paradox is that those who like to be considered leaders according to false human standards are actually without authority (1:22), while those who make themselves servants are truly great (10:43). From a literary standpoint, the issue here is not the superiority of Christianity over Judaism, but the superiority of God's authority (evident in Jesus) over false human authority (exemplified by the religious leaders). Jesus sometimes refers to gentile rulers as illustrative of false authority as well (10:33, 42).

The same principle may be applied to Matthew. It is an unfortunate but incontestable fact that, over the years, Matthew's Gospel has aroused in many readers not only antipathy toward the religious leaders as characters in the story, but also hostility for Jewish people and their leaders in general. From the perspective of narrative criticism, however, such a reading represents a gross example of the referential fallacy and completely misses the point of the story. The religious leaders in Matthew's narrative do not "stand for" any real people in the world *outside the story*, but are constructs of the implied author designed to fulfill a particular role *in the story*. Regardless of whether they were modeled after real people known to the real author, their current function as characters in a story is not referential but poetic. They are emblematic of the forces of evil that God through Christ is able to overcome. The literary effect of Matthew's portrayal is to impress upon the reader that God, in Christ, has overcome evil, even though it succeeded at doing its worst. If Matthew softened his characterization of the leaders, made them less evil than they appear, the force with which this point is made would be weakened. And, since in Matthew's story world the religious leaders *are* evil, Matthew certainly does not want the reader to feel any sympathy for them; to do so would be to encourage sympathy with evil itself. The modern reader may, of course, object to the use of such a device, but once it is recognized that it *is* a device, the story becomes easier to interpret.

In Luke's story, as we have seen, the implied reader is actually moved to feel sympathy for the religious leaders instead of the intense antipathy created in Matthew's narrative. According to narrative criticism, this should not be construed as evidence that Luke was less "anti-Semitic" than Matthew or explained in any terms that involve suppositions about the real author. Rather, Luke tells his story differently because he has a different point to make. In Luke's narrative, the religious leaders contribute to the overall effect of the narrative by demonstrating a tragic response to the protagonist Jesus, who nevertheless refuses to give up hope for them. The intention of God evident in the ministry of Jesus throughout Luke is not to defeat enemies but to reclaim them. Luke's version of the conflict presents the mission of Christ not as a triumph over evil but as a divine offer of grace, peace, and reconciliation. If Luke sometimes makes the leaders look bad, it is not to highlight the greatness of Christ's victory in defeating them, but the greatness of his mercy in forgiving them. Accordingly, the impact of Luke's story on the implied reader is every bit as profound as Matthew's, but it is a different impact. The lasting images in this story are of Jesus weeping over his enemies' failure to accept the peace he brings (19:41-44) and, finally, of Jesus nailed to the cross, praying, still, for their forgiveness.

6

Settings

Settings represent that aspect of narrative that provides context for the actions of the characters. Every theater-goer knows the significance of settings for drama: some productions are staged with elaborate scenery while for others the decor is intentionally sparse. Since even a bare stage counts as a set, however, it is impossible to imagine a play without any setting at all. In the same way, settings in literature are as integral to the story as are the events and the characters themselves.[1]

These basic elements of a story may also be compared to the grammatical components of English sentence structure. Events correspond roughly to verbs, for in them the story's action is expressed. Characters are like nouns, for they perform these actions or, perhaps, are acted upon. Character traits may be likened to adjectives since they describe the characters involved in the action. And settings? Settings are the adverbs of literary structure: they designate when, where, and how the action occurs.

Chatman says the demarcation between settings and characters (both of which he calls "existents") is not a simple line but a continuum.[2] The crowds in our Gospel narratives, for instance, sometimes speak and act as characters, but at other times they blend into the background. They are simply there, as part of the context within which the characters must act. How can we determine whether to treat such crowds as characters or as settings? It seems that Chatman misses one point of distinction: unlike characters, settings are never presented as espousing a particular point of view. Some of the confusion Chatman notes occurs with regard to traits. Settings may be "characterized" as possessing certain descriptive qualities: the sea in *Moby Dick* is "hostile." To the extent that such traits are ascribed to settings, the latter may seem "character-like." The ascription of traits, however, is only one part of the process of characterization. There is no thought in *Moby Dick* that the sea actually evinces a hostile attitude toward the characters. If it did (as it sometimes does in fairy tales, for example) it would cross the line and become a character itself. Similarly, the crowds in our Gospel narratives should be treated as characters when they are represented as espousing a particular point of view.

Settings resemble characters in one other respect. They too are not limited to the functional role they serve in the story but have the capacity to transcend that role. Some settings (such as Camelot, the Garden of Eden, or the Land of Oz) become so clearly entrenched in the mind of the reader that they, like memorable characters, take on a life of their own. The reader can easily imagine events not reported in the narrative occurring within these settings. Of course all settings, like all characters, are the creation of the implied author. As such, the immediate interest of narrative criticism is in the role that settings serve within the narrative itself.

A NARRATIVE UNDERSTANDING OF SETTINGS

Settings serve a variety of functions. They may be symbolic. They may help to reveal characters, determine conflict, or provide structure for the story.[3] Chatman notes that a chief function of settings is "to contribute to the mood of the narrative."[4] As with characters and events, it is possible to evaluate the significance of settings: some are irrelevant to the plot of the story while others are highly charged with meaning and importance.

Abrams defines settings as related to locale, time, and social circumstances.[5] Accordingly, we will consider three types of settings: spatial, temporal, and social.

Spatial Settings

Settings that pertain to location or space are the most widely discussed in literary theory. They include the physical environment in which the characters of the story live as well as the "props" and "furniture" that make up that environment, such as articles of clothing, modes of transportation, and so on.

Mieke Bal suggests that one dynamic frequently relevant for spatial settings of stories is the contrast between inside and outside.[6] Inside settings sometimes carry the connotation of protection or security, but they may also suggest confinement. Likewise, outside settings may connote danger in one narrative and freedom in another. This possibility for different connotations opens the door for paradox, and many stories have seized upon the notion of equating security with confinement or danger with freedom. The same type of opposition can be detected in contrasts between country and city, solitude and society, or land and sea.

In keeping with structuralist theory, Bal emphasizes the special role that boundaries play in mediating between opposed locations. Doors, for example, exercise a mediating role between inside and outside. In the novel *Robinson Crusoe*, an island mediates between the usual associations of land and sea: ostensibly a place of confinement, it becomes for the protagonist a place of freedom. The importance of boundaries can also be observed in the Gospel of Mark, as in the frequent instances of Jesus teaching people by the shore of the Sea of Galilee. At one point, Mark even describes Jesus as teaching from a boat (4:1). Thus, Jesus himself is pictured as being on the sea, while the crowd remains on the land. Such images are fraught with possibility for mediation between spatial opposites. The connotation of such a spatial setting may reflect mediation that is going on at other levels of the narrative as well.

In some literature, description of locale appears to become an end in itself. Narratives sometimes expend a great many words depicting environs in detail not required for the story itself. Thus, the implied author hopes to create a literary equivalent of a landscape painting, a work that engenders images that have an evocative power all their own.[7] The use of description in our Gospel narratives is much more reserved. Spatial settings are presented with only scant notation: "Jerusalem," "a mountain," "the temple." The reader is given no information about such places that is not directly relevant to the plot.

There is a similar paucity of sensory data. Information regarding spatial aspects of settings is usually communicated in terms related to our senses.[8] If the Gospels were more like modern novels we would probably read about the sound of "waves lapping at the shore of the Sea of Galilee" and the feel of "coarse, dry sand trod underfoot in the Judean desert." Such luxury of narration is not to be found. Textures, sounds, smells, and tastes are usually left to our imagination.

Robert Funk has noted that such brevity of description is remarkable even for literature of the time.[9] The writings of Josephus,

71

which are roughly contemporary with our Gospels, contain long descriptive passages. In *The Jewish War*, for instance, a detailed account of the temple in Jerusalem includes description of its foundations, dimensions, and furnishings (5:148ff). In the Gospels, we would not even know that the temple area had tables in it if Jesus did not happen to overturn them in the course of the story.

In short, description of spatial settings in the Gospels seems limited to dramatic and utilitarian effect. Scenery is only important insofar as it affects specified actions of the characters. This may mean, on the one hand, that the reader's role in conceptualizing the world of the story is less restricted and the possibility of different readers experiencing the story in different ways is enhanced. On the other hand, it may also mean that the narrative assumes certain perceptions on the part of the implied reader that do not come automatically to real readers today. When the Gospel of Mark reports the rending of the temple curtain at Jesus' death (15:38) in a manner reminiscent of the rending of the heavens at his baptism (1:10), the implied author may be assuming his reader knows what Josephus tells us outright, namely, that the temple curtain was in fact a tapestry on which the heavens were pictorially displayed.[10] Finally, the lack of description that typifies most references to spatial settings in these narratives calls special attention to such information when it is provided: the purple clothing of the rich man (Luke 16:19); the five porticoes of the Bethzatha pool (John 5:2); the sound of the mighty rushing wind (Acts 2:2). The reader expects such descriptions to be significant.

Temporal Settings

References to temporal settings are of at least two types: *chronological* and *typological*. Chronological references may be further classed as either *locative* or *durative*. Locative references specify the particular point in time in which a given action takes place. This location in time may be broad (the year or the century) or narrow (the day or the hour). The Gospel of Luke locates a now famous decree that went out from Caesar Augustus in the time "when Quirinius was governor of Syria" (2:1-2). Similarly, in Mark's passion narrative, we are told that "it was the third hour" when Jesus was crucified (15:25).

Durative references also indicate a chronological temporal setting, but they denote an interval of time. In John's Gospel, Jesus' opponents tell him that the Jerusalem temple was built over a period of 46 years

(2:20). The temporal reference does not indicate the point in time when the temple was constructed but the amount of time that transpired during its building. Likewise, a woman whom Jesus heals in Mark is said to have had a flow of blood "for 12 years" (5:25).

Typological references, finally, indicate the kind of time within which an action transpires. When the narrator of John's Gospel says that Nicodemus came to Jesus "by night" (3:2), he does not mean to indicate when the meeting occurred (which night?) but rather to inform us that it was night at the time. These references usually assume contrast: they specify one kind of time as opposed to another (night, not day). In Mark 13:18, Jesus tells his disciples to pray that the great tribulation to come will not happen "in winter" (as opposed to "in summer"). Similarly, when the Gospels specify the temporal setting for something Jesus does as being "on the Sabbath," the point may not be to locate when in story time the event occurred so much as to specify what kind of time it was when the event occurred.[11]

References to temporal settings in our Gospels are typically as brief as descriptions of the spatial environment.[12] Once again, then, the descriptions that do occur receive all the more emphasis due to their rarity. Such references may be rich in connotative significance. With regard to Nicodemus, "nighttime" suggests a desire for secrecy, but also, perhaps, a need to be enlightened (John 3:2, 19-21). "Wintertime" is considered more arduous than summertime and so serves as a fitting metaphor for apocalyptic travail. "Sabbathtime" connotes rest and reverence but is given fuller content within these narratives as a time provided by God for the meeting of human need.

Such obvious implications of certain temporal settings invite closer examination of others. Why does Mark tell us that the woman in 5:25 had experienced a flow of blood "for 12 years"? Is the number 12 symbolic, recalling perhaps the 12 tribes of Israel? Is there any connection with the 12 baskets of food collected by the disciples later in the narrative (6:43; 8:19)? Or is the reference ironic, insofar as it presents Jesus as being accosted by a woman who has bled for 12 years while on his way to heal another woman who is only 12 years old (5:42)?[13] Narrative critics cannot assume that all temporal references and settings possess meaning beyond their literal function in the story, but the scarcity with which such references occur in our Gospels does suggest that they are not used without relevance.

It is also possible to speak of temporal settings in narrative in a broader, more comprehensive sense. Paul Ricoeur distinguishes between *mortal time* and *monumental time*.[14] All the references we have discussed so far fall under what he calls mortal time, the time in which the characters of a story live out their lives, just as people do in the real world. Mortal time is measured by calendars, watches, clocks, and sundials. Monumental time, on the other hand, refers to the broad sweep of time that includes but also transcends history. It cannot be measured either by people in the real world or by characters in a story. Nevertheless, people have some sense of what they think it is like. Some cultures have perceived of time as linear, others as circular, spiral, or concentric. Narratives embody a certain vision of monumental time, just as they embody a particular worldview. In some narratives (such as those that begin with the words, "Once upon a time . . .") the view of time is notably ahistorical. In our Gospels, this is not the case. Luke's reference to the decree of Caesar Augustus is more detailed than anything in Matthew, Mark, or John, but each of these narratives presents a particular view of history as the stage on which its drama unfolds.

The narrative representation of time found in our Gospels has often been studied in theological categories of salvation history. A literary investigation of temporal settings, especially those associated with monumental time, may duplicate these traditional studies in some ways, since both are interested in elucidating the vision of time assumed by the narrative.

Social Settings

The third aspect of settings to be considered concerns what Abrams calls social circumstances. These include the political institutions, class structures, economic systems, social customs, and general cultural context assumed to be operative in the work.

Identification of social settings is especially important in ancient literature, because so much of the context is not immediately accessible to the understanding of real readers today. Nevertheless, some scholars have shied away from discussion of such settings in literary studies of the Gospels, perhaps because they feel it is more appropriate to the domain of historical analysis. As Rhoads indicates, however, using knowledge of the history and culture of the first century as an aid in understanding a particular Gospel's story world is quite a different matter from using story elements to reconstruct historical events.[15] Other scholars, in recognition of the necessity of such information for literary analysis, have coined hyphenated terms for their methodologies, calling them socio-literary or socio-narratological approaches.

Such prefixes are actually unnecessary, since attention to social settings is intrinsic to narrative criticism, properly understood.

In secular literary criticism, there is no such embarrassment. Scholars recognize that literature is not comprehensible without some understanding of the cultural phenomena assumed by the text. It would be insufficient to identify the setting of *Uncle Tom's Cabin* as a plantation outside New Orleans in the mid-19th century. Another essential aspect of this book's setting is the social institution of slavery that was practiced at the time. Without some knowledge of that institution, the story cannot be understood, at least not in the manner expected of the implied reader.

Similarly, the social setting of Luke 7:36-50 is a meal, but the circumstances of this meal are unlike those of meals enjoyed by modern readers. Jesus criticizes his host for not washing his feet, kissing him, or anointing his head with oil. The reader is expected to understand that such lapses of hospitality imply a lack of love. During the course of the meal, a woman enters the room, weeps at the feet of Jesus (who is lying down to eat), and then proceeds to dry his feet with her hair. The modern reader is not likely to understand the revulsion with which this behavior is regarded in the text without some knowledge of first-century social customs. The woman, of course, is a prostitute, but even this recognition is shortsighted if the reader evaluates it in terms of modern ideas about prostitution.

CASE STUDY: SETTINGS IN THE GOSPEL OF MARK

In order to demonstrate how a literary approach to settings works in practice, we will now concentrate on the settings of one particular narrative, the Gospel of Mark.

Spatial Settings in Mark

Rhoads and Michie briefly discuss the significance of key Markan settings in their study, *Mark As Story*.[16] The symbolic function of these settings usually derives from what Wheelwright would call ancestral vitality (see chapter 3 above). Specifically, local settings are imbued with meaning through association with events in Israel's past. The Jordan River, the site of John's baptism, served previously as the threshold for Israel's entrance into "the promised land." The desert or wilderness is a place of testing for Jesus (40 days) just as it was for Israel (40 years) in the Hebrew Scriptures. The sea is a threatening place of chaos and destruction, producing sudden storms that recall the chaos of the waters in Israel's creation story or the devastating effects of the great flood. Similarly, Jesus' divine authority over the sea recalls the parting of the waters by God at creation and at the exodus. The mountain is a place of refuge, safety, and revelation, a role that it also plays in stories about Moses and Elijah—both of whom appear with Jesus on a mountain in 9:4.

Elizabeth Struthers Malbon finds three types of spatial settings in Mark: *geopolitical* settings, such as regions, cities, and towns; *topographical* settings, such as physical features of the earth; and *architectural* settings, such as houses and synagogues.[17] This threefold classification corresponds roughly to Bal's contrast of outside settings to inside ones. Malbon, however, subdivides the outside settings into geopolitical and topographical categories.

With regard to geopolitical settings, a basic distinction can be made between those that belong to the Jewish homeland and those that represent foreign lands. The Jewish homeland, furthermore, actually comprises both Galilee and Judea, which are treated quite differently in Mark's story.[18] Jesus himself is from Galilee and it is in Galilee that he calls his disciples and conducts the bulk of his ministry. Judea (especially Jerusalem) is the provenance of his opponents (3:22; 7:1) and the site of his passion. His disciples are instructed to return to Galilee after the Passion, just as Jesus himself will do (14:28; 16:7).

The underlying theme that Malbon detects here is a contrast between the "familiar" and the "strange." The Jewish homeland is more familiar than the strange foreign lands, but by the same token, Galilee is more familiar than Judea. In the latter portion of Mark's story the contrast can be pushed a step further, for some parts of Judea (e.g., Bethany, the Mount of Olives, and Gethsemane) are more familiar than Jerusalem itself. Attention to the connotations of such settings aids the reader in understanding Mark's story. The Sea of Galilee, for example, serves as a "boundary" between the homeland and the foreign lands; people who seek to cross this boundary often meet with resistance (4:37; 5:48). Similarly, when Jesus instructs his disciples about the coming tribulation, he is described as sitting "on the Mount of Olives opposite the temple" (13:3).

In the case of topographical settings, the basic distinction is between heaven and earth. Settings related to earth may be divided into land and sea, and the settings on land are subject to further classification according to whether they represent isolated areas (such as the wilderness) or inhabited areas (such as cities, towns, or marketplaces).

The schematic theme underlying these topographical oppositions is the contrast of promise and threat. Heaven represents promise in Mark's story. God's Spirit and voice come from heaven (1:10, 11; 9:7) and it is to heaven that characters look for an experience of God's power (6:41; 7:34). Characters fall to the earth, on the other hand, when they are beset by sickness or sorrow (9:20; 14:35). The promise of treasure in heaven is contrasted with the danger of maintaining treasure on earth (10:21). Similar connotations hold for other topographical distinctions. The normal and secure environment of the land is opposed to the threatening danger of the sea, and isolated areas serve as places of refuge to which Jesus retreats from the stress and danger of inhabited regions (1:53; 6:31).

Just as a shoreline or a boat can mediate between the opposition of land and sea, so also mountains can mediate between heaven and earth. Mountains are closer to heaven than the rest of the earth and so are an ideal place for prayer (6:46) and revelation (9:2). Notably, it is "to the mountains" that residents of Judea are to flee when the great tribulation comes (13:14). In another sense, however, Mark's story does not view the opposition between heaven and earth as being mediated, but as being ultimately surpassed by the power of Jesus' words: "Heaven and earth will pass away, but my words will not pass away" (13:31).

When Malbon considers the architectural settings in Mark's story she discovers a thematic contrast between space that is logically sacred and that which is profane. Buildings may be said to be more sacred than tombs, which are obviously profane. But buildings may be subdivided into religious structures and residential ones; a temple or a synagogue would logically be regarded as more sacred than a palace or a house. According to Malbon, however, Mark's treatment of these architectural settings is surprising. The temple is condemned as a "den of robbers" (11:17) and houses become the principal site for teaching and healing. God's greatest work of all occurs not in the temple, or in any building, but in a tomb (16:1-8). Thus, Mark's story assigns a more positive value to those architectural spaces closest to the profane pole. Ultimately, however, the point may be that no space can contain what is truly sacred, for the tomb does not hold Jesus either. The empty tomb, the ruined temple, and the reconstitution of the house as a place for teaching and healing all bear witness to what Malbon identifies as a breakdown of any opposition of sacred and profane in Mark's story.

Rhoads and Michie, Malbon, and others have also called attention to the patterns of movement in Mark's story described as "the way." Journeys often play a prominent role in literature, from Homer's *Odyssey* to Dante's *Divine Comedy* to J. R. R. Tolkien's *The Lord of the Rings*. In Mark's Gospel Jesus' travels are sometimes less important than the simple fact that he is traveling. In this sense, the journey itself becomes a setting.

Mark uses the term *way* a total of 16 times. At the beginning of the story, John "prepares the way" for Jesus (1:2, 3). Jesus not only travels throughout Galilee and beyond, but also sends his disciples "on the way" (6:8). Then Jesus sets out "on the way" to Jerusalem (10:32) where, when he arrives, he is hypocritically flattered as one who "teaches the way of God" (20:21). Rhoads and Michie believe "the way" in Mark is actually a metaphor for the way of God.[19] Being on the way means more than simply moving through a physical landscape but signifies moving toward the goal that God has set. We know from other sources that the term *way* was actually used as a self-designation for the early Christian movement (cf. Acts 9:2). Even within Mark's story, however, the way signifies a movement on the part of Jesus' disciples toward understanding and acceptance of what Jesus represents. Jesus is described as "going ahead" of his disciples on the way and they are described as following in some amazement (10:32). In another instance, Jesus asks them what they have been discussing "on the way" and they are too ashamed to confess that, ironically, their concern "on the way" has been with their own prestige and privilege (4:33-34).

Temporal Settings in Mark

Since the whole story of Mark's Gospel is set in motion by the words, "the time is fulfilled!" (1:14), it should be obvious that time is of great significance in this narrative.[20] Such a reference concerns what Ricoeur calls monumental time. But Mark's reader also needs to attend to everyday temporal settings (i.e., "mortal time"); it seems to make a difference in this narrative whether events occur "in the morning," "on the Sabbath," or "during the Passover."

We will speak first about Mark's concept of monumental time. Dan Via notes that, in the course of Mark's narrative, there are temporal references to both "the beginning" (10:6; 13:9) and "the end" (13:7, 13).[21] If time is thought to have both a beginning and an end, then it must also have a middle. Mark does not explicitly refer to "the middle" of time, but Via believes this is the overall temporal setting that is assumed for Mark's story.

As Via explains it, Mark's concept of time includes a theme common in Jewish apocalyptic literature, namely, the idea that the end will involve a new beginning. In fact, the end should in some way correspond to the beginning. Theologically, this is grounded in the notion that God is first and last, the one who declares the end from the beginning (cf. Isa. 40:10; 48:12), the author of both creation and new creation. In less overtly theological terms, literary critic Gerard Genette has observed that a "first time" is always also a "last time," insofar as the newness, spontaneity, life, and intensity of original experience cannot be repeated.[22] In the same way, the role of the last time is to be once again the first time, to recover what the beginning has lost in the middle. Such recovery does not consist of repetition of events (for that may be exactly what happens in the middle), but of restoration of power and vitality.

The temporal setting of Mark's story is the middle of time. At the story's outset, however, Jesus announces that "the time is fulfilled!" This eschatological declaration marks an anticipatory actualization of the end, which for Mark is also an actualization of the beginning. Therefore, when Jesus is questioned about divorce, he responds by affirming that "from the beginning" marriage has been indissoluble (10:6). He recognizes that Moses allowed divorce because of "hardness of heart" (10:5), which is a reality in the middle of time (cf. 3:5; 6:52; 8:17), but he expects people to live now as though they were in the beginning before hardness of heart set in. Elsewhere in Mark, Jesus calls people to live in the belief that the end-time rule of God is a present reality. This apparent paradox is resolved by an understanding of Mark's concept of monumental time: the in-breaking of the end represents a recovery of the beginning. For people in the middle of time who experience such an in-breaking, both end and beginning are supremely relevant.

When we turn to a consideration of mortal time, we find the Markan settings are distinctive. Chronological time in Mark's story is measured in days rather than in weeks or months or years. Mark makes no references to seasons or holidays (save for one Passover) that might mark an extended passing of time. On the other hand, we are frequently told that evening falls or that morning comes, events that mark the passing of individual days. Indeed, nothing happens in this story that requires a larger unit of measurement. Jesus is in the wilderness "forty days" (1:13). He returns to Capernaum "after some days" (2:1). A crowd remains with him "for three days" (8:2). He teaches that he will rise from the dead "after three days" (8:31). He is transfigured on the mountain "after six days" (9:2). The Passover is reported to be coming "after two days" (14:1). He is accused of claiming he will rebuild the temple "in three days" (14:58; 15:29).[23] Mark's preference for measuring time in days even affects idiomatic references to the future; the expression used most often for describing the future is "in those days" (1:9; 2:20; 8:1; 13:17; 13:19; 13:24; cf. 2:20; 13:20; 14:25).

This reckoning of chronology in terms of days lends an urgency to Mark's story that is reinforced by his frequent use of the word "immediately" (more than 40 times) and by the opening declaration that "time has been fulfilled" (1:14).[24] In the passion narrative, furthermore, this sense of immediacy is heightened as the story suddenly shifts to marking time not in days but in *hours*. Jesus prays that "this hour might pass" (14:35), rebukes his disciples for failing to watch with him "for one hour" (14:37), and finally declares that "the hour has come" (14:41). The story of the crucifixion itself is narrated with reference to the third hour (15:25), the sixth hour (15:33), and the ninth hour (15:34). Notably, the only exception to what was just said concerning idiomatic references to the future is found in a prediction Jesus makes regarding the passion that awaits his disciples. He refers to this occasion not with the usual expression, "in that day," but with the novel phrase, "in that hour" (13:11). Perhaps the most important point regarding the future, however, is that all time (days and hours) belongs to the province of God: "Of that day or that hour no one knows, not even the angels in heaven, nor the Son, but only the Father" (13:32).

Since chronological temporal settings in Mark are almost exclusively limited to days and hours, it should not be surprising to learn that the most prominent typological temporal settings are periods of the day: evening, night, and morning. They should be considered in this order because, in the Jewish frame of reference, a day is thought to begin at sunset (evening) rather than at sunrise (morning).

One might imagine that evening would be a time of winding down, of completing tasks and finding relaxation. In Mark's story, however, this is not the case. Evening can be a time of great activity, even of starting new ventures. It is in the evening that "the whole city" of Capernaum gathers at Jesus' door, where he heals the sick and exorcises demons (1:32-34). Twice, Jesus' disciples set out on trips in the evening, trips that are intended to inaugurate major new phases in the ministry

(4:36; 6:47). Evening is sometimes presented as a time of preparation. Jesus visits the temple one evening (11:11) in preparation for his assault on that institution the next day (11:15). On Passover evening, he shares a meal with his disciples that anticipates his impending death (14:22-24) and the coming reign of God (14:25). Most telling of all is the statement that Jesus is laid in the tomb on the evening of "the day of Preparation" (15:42). Indeed, Jesus' burial does not so much conclude the Passion story in Mark as it prepares for the resurrection narrative in 16:1-8. In short, the connotation of "evening" in Mark's story is one of beginnings, not endings.

Night is a time of trouble, turmoil, and danger in Mark's story. Never is it a time for rest (cf. 13:35-37). "In the fourth watch of the night" Jesus comes to his disciples when they are "making headway painfully," beset by storms at sea (6:48). Also at night, Jesus is arrested and deserted by his disciples. Mark calls attention to the temporal setting in Jesus' words to Peter: "This very night, before the cock crows twice, you will deny me three times." The same may also be true of 14:27 ("you will all fall away this night"), though the textual status of this verse is uncertain.

Mornings, like evenings, are a time of beginning and preparation in Mark. For Jesus, morning is a time of prayer (1:35). For the religious leaders, it is a time to act swiftly; after a midnight trial, they have Jesus delivered to Pilate "as soon as it is morning" (15:1). Sometimes morning brings new insight. In the morning the disciples discover that the fig tree Jesus cursed the previous day is now withered (11:20). "Very early" in the morning the women discover the empty tomb (16:2-8). In such instances, the morning perspective interprets preparatory events of previous evenings (11:11; 15:42) while introducing new beginnings that are preparatory in themselves.

We can see a correlation between Mark's treatment of evening, nighttime, and morning and his overall concept of monumental time. The typological character of night in Mark's story is similar to his understanding of the middle of time. It is a period marked by hardness of heart and apostasy, a time of trouble in which it is difficult to make headway but important to keep watch. On either side of this period, however, there are times marked by beginnings and new beginnings, times that seem linked in destiny and purpose. Just as Mark envisions the end-time as encroaching upon the middle, so the morning has a way of creeping into the night. In 1:35, Mark says that Jesus rises to pray "in the morning, during the night," a reference that is paradoxical to say the least. Such an overlapping of night and morning in terms of mortal time expresses metaphorically the same thought that is declared elsewhere with regard to monumental time, which can be said to be fulfilled even before the end has fully come (1:14). The resurrection, we remember, is discovered *very early* when the sun has barely risen (16:2). We are to assume that this greatest of new beginnings must have actually occurred at some point while it was still night.[25]

Mark's overriding concern regarding temporal settings is to emphasize that all time belongs to God. We observed earlier that chronological times (days and hours) are known to the Father and the most significant of these, only to the Father (13:32). In the same way, God's rule is active "night and day" in ways that are often unknown (4:26-27). The directive to people who live in the middle of time is to keep watch during every kind of time: "in the evening," "at midnight," "at cock-crow," and "in the morning" (13:35). All time belongs to God and God's new beginning may come suddenly at any time.

Social Settings in Mark

Space is too short here to provide all the historical, sociological, and cultural data necessary to understand the social circumstances underlying Mark's story.[26] Still, a few brief points are worth noting.

The political setting for Mark's story is that of a conquered land. Political authority is in the hands of despised foreign rulers, like Herod (6:14-29) and Pilate (15:1-15). The difficulty of living under such a regime informs Mark's narrative explicitly at several points (e.g., 10:42; 12:13-17; 13:9) and may also be significant in passages that are not obviously political. We might consider, for example, what nuances the implied reader would impute to the name "Legion" used for a host of demons that have possessed a man (5:9). In the political setting assumed for Mark's story, the term *legion* was used to refer to a military unit of the occupying Roman army.[27]

One aspect of these political tensions especially significant for Mark's story is the presence of resistance movements fostered by them. These include such triumphalist causes as Zealotism, messianism, and millenialism.[28] Mark's story envisions a world populated with false prophets and false messiahs (13:22). Jesus himself avoids public identification as "the messiah," at least initially (8:30). It is not until after he has been anointed *for burial* (14:8) that he openly accepts the designation Messiah, which means "Anointed One." Even then, the title is to be understood in terms of divine sonship and authority rather than human political aspirations (14:61-62).

The social setting of Mark's story is a class society, in the eyes of which some people are more important than others. The Gentile rulers and the Jewish religious leaders in Mark's story obviously presume to be at the top of such a status pyramid, while tax collectors, prostitutes, lepers, and beggars are all at the bottom. The world of Mark's story is also decidedly patriarchal, placing little value on women and even less on children. Mark's implied reader is expected to regard such perceptions as "givens" and, so, to be shocked by the behavior and attitude of Jesus when he ignores or even reverses this ideology. For example, when an important Jewish man asks Jesus to heal his daughter (5:23), the reader fully expects Jesus to comply (as he does), but it is by no means a foregone conclusion that Jesus will also assist a Gentile woman who comes to him with a similar request (7:26). Many modern Bible readers consider Mark 7:24-30 a difficult passage on account of Jesus' initial hesitation to help the woman in need. For Mark's implied reader, however, the difficult part of this passage is not Jesus' hesitation but the fact that ultimately the help is given. Mark's narrative is filled with such surprises for readers who think the way the story assumes its readers will think.

Conclusions on Settings in Mark

This discussion has attempted to describe in a rudimentary fashion the places, times, and circumstances within which characters act and events transpire in Mark's narrative. Much of the material in this section has resembled traditional historical-critical studies more closely than that of previous chapters. This is because the geographical, temporal, and social settings of the Gospels have always been concerns of historical criticism.

How is the literary approach different? We have tried here to elucidate these settings as they contribute to an understanding of the narrative as story, not history. We have been interested, for example, in the metaphorical and connotative value that such settings receive within the narrative. The narrative settings discussed here might also serve as clues to understanding the historical settings of the Gospel's real author. For example, many scholars believe that Mark's positive evaluation of Galilee is best explained by presuming that his own community is located there. Such suppositions, however, move beyond the immediate concerns of narrative criticism.

7

Story as
Scripture

When some people encounter books with titles like *Mark As Story* or *Luke's Passion Account As Literature*,[1] they may be reminded of "Bible As Literature" classes offered by some colleges, universities, and public high schools. But there is a difference. The emphasis in courses taught at secular institutions is normally on studying the Bible as literature *instead of* as Scripture. The focus is on pure literary and aesthetic evaluation, not theological interpretation. Books like those mentioned above, however, attempt to understand the Bible as Scripture and literature at the same time. The intention is to read the Bible as Scripture in story form.

The advent of such an approach is not without hermeneutical implication. The question is asked, What effect will the use of this method have on the wider task of interpreting Scripture for the life of the church? Both potential benefits and possible pitfalls have been perceived. In this chapter, we will enumerate frequently cited examples of each and will consider the extent to which they are justified. Both praise and criticism tend to be exaggerated when this method is evaluated by way of comparison with other approaches. Our goal is simply to recognize what narrative criticism *can* do and what it *cannot* do, without pitting it defensively (or offensively) against other methodologies.

THE BENEFITS OF NARRATIVE CRITICISM

1. *Narrative criticism focuses on the text of Scripture itself.* For many, the great appeal of this method is that it is text-centered, seeking to understand the Bible on its own terms rather than in reference to

something else. As such, it is said to satisfy a desire often voiced by students of religion to "spend less time studying *about* the Bible and more time studying the Bible *itself*." Effective use of narrative criticism, however, demands knowledge of the social and historical circumstances assumed by the narrative. The method does not really allow one to escape the need to learn "about the Bible." Still, it is true that the process of narrative criticism does involve a deep absorption into the world of the text. In a sense, the text serves as its own context; passages are read in light of the total narrative without regard for discernment of previous source strata or stages of composition. The critic who follows this approach spends most of his or her time actually reading and rereading the text, reflecting upon what it means in light of its own narrative context.

2. *Narrative criticism provides some insight into biblical texts for which the historical background is uncertain*. In the past century, an enormous amount of research has been devoted to questions regarding the authorship, dating, provenance, and sources of various New Testament books. Nevertheless, the cases in which anything like a consensus has been reached are few. An advantage of narrative criticism is that it enables scholars to learn much about the meaning and impact of certain books without first having to settle these persistent and perhaps unsolvable problems. For example, consider the much-debated "synoptic problem": Did Matthew and Luke use Mark as a source or did Mark write last and abridge the other two Gospels? Most redaction critics have found it necessary to assume a particular solution to this query and then proceed to interpret the material accordingly. The advantage of narrative criticism is that it begins with a given (the narrative) rather than with a hypothesis. William Farmer, who is not otherwise an advocate of this approach, has agreed that literary criticism provides a way around the impasse of source theories that biblical scholars currently face. He suggests that such approaches will be useful "for the interim" until a better understanding of the historical origins of this material is obtained.[2]

3. *Narrative criticism provides for checks and balances on traditional methods*. If a literary reading is basically compatible with a particular historical interpretation, it may be viewed as corroborating the accuracy of the latter. On the other hand, if the meaning of a text as literature is perceived as radically inconsistent with traditional interpretations, then scholars in both fields will want to reconsider their evaluation of evidence. Historical critics, for example, have often held

that Mark portrays the disciples in a negative way because he is po-
lemicizing against people claimed as forebears by rival Christian communities.[3] By itself, narrative criticism does not inquire into the
historical intentions of a work's real author, but some narrative critics
believe that the effect of Mark's portrayal is to arouse sympathy for the
disciples on the part of the reader rather than animosity or hostility.
Accordingly, if historical critics still wish to maintain that Mark intended
to polemicize against the original disciples of Jesus, they may now have
to decide that he also "botched the job" and accidently created a
narrative that has almost the opposite effect. While such incompetence
is not impossible, many scholars now view the polemical explanation
for Mark's portrayal of the disciples as less viable than before. The
search for an alternative definition of Mark's intention has begun.[4]

4. *Narrative criticism tends to bring scholars and nonprofessional
Bible readers closer together.* It has been said that the historical-critical
method took the Bible out of the hands of the general reader and placed
it under the auspices of "a papacy of scholars."[5] This complaint is lodged
against historical critics who seem to operate with the presupposition
that the Bible cannot be properly understood without specialized
knowledge of the origin, transmission, and editorial revision of its
contents. Narrative criticism is praised for seeking to interpret the text
from the perspective of its implied reader, who is not expected to know
anything about the history of the text's transmission or to be able to
reconstruct the *Sitze im Leben* that passages served before being incorporated into the narrative as a whole.

It is true that scholarly interpretations offered by narrative critics
sometimes match what untrained readers have assumed the text to
mean all along. Such confirmation of insight is not to be despised.
Many regard it as a welcome humbling of scholarship—a voluntary
rejection of fascination with the esoteric and a restoration of respect
for what Hans Frei called "the plain sense" of Scripture.[6] Still, this
perceived benefit of narrative criticism can be overstated and exaltation
of the discipline over historical criticism on this account is unfair. It
would be naive to expect the perspective of a Gospel's implied reader
to always match that of modern readers today. Matthew's implied reader, for example, apparently regards the social institution of slavery as
acceptable (8:9; 10:24-25). Accordingly, nonprofessional Bible readers
who appreciate the goals of narrative criticism should rely on the guidance of scholars trained in the discipline for determining the perspective
from which a text is to be read. In this regard, narrative criticism is

87

no different from historical methods; untrained Bible readers who appreciate the goals of historical criticism also welcome the guidance that scholars trained in that methodology are able to provide.

5. *Narrative criticism stands in a close relationship to the believing community.* Interpreting biblical passages in terms of their intended literary effect rather than their apparent historical reference sometimes salvages material that would otherwise be difficult for members of believing communities to accept. The presence of mythological and supernatural elements, which has troubled modern interpreters for decades, ceases to be a problem.[7] The horrid anti-Jewish passages in Matthew's Gospel provide another example. No matter how disturbing such passages sound to us today, narrative critics are able to demonstrate that the intended literary effect of Matthew's story is not to foster anti-Semitism.[8]

This method also treats texts in a manner that is consistent with a Christian understanding of canon. The Christian church has always confessed Scripture itself to be authoritative rather than the oral traditions or primary sources that stand behind Scripture. By focusing on the finished form of the text, narrative criticism seeks to interpret Scripture at its canonical level; the text that is considered is identical with that which believing communities identify as authoritative for their faith and practice. In addition, narrative criticism emphasizes a Christian doctrine of the Spirit. Since revelation is considered to be an event that happens now, through an interaction of the reader with the text, an active role for the Spirit is crucial to the process of interpretation.

This apparent compatibility between the goals of narrative criticism and the interests of believing communities is especially attractive to those who have been uncomfortable with the challenges posed by historical criticism. Although the historical-critical method has produced (and continues to produce) innumerable insights for communities of faith, the relationship between the historical consciousness that this method requires and the faith of those on whose behalf it is employed has never been an easy one. As Alan Culpepper puts it, "Historical investigation demands skepticism and offers in the end only a reconstruction of the evidence that is more or less probable."[9] Such skepticism is a far cry from the certainty of faith with which the Gospel narratives appear to have been written and with which they obviously expect to be read. By interpreting texts from the point of view of their own implied readers, narrative criticism offers exegesis that is inevitably from a faith perspective.

We should be careful, however, not to disparage historical criticism simply because it raises questions that are difficult for people of faith. The struggles that historical-critical investigation engender are significant for theological growth. Employment of narrative criticism as a means of avoiding difficult or controversial issues represents, in my mind, a misuse of the methodology. Mature theological reflection demands both appreciation for the faith perspective evident in the implied readers of our Gospels and consideration for the skepticism demanded by modern historical consciousness.

6. *Narrative criticism offers potential for bringing believing communities together.* Narrative criticism invites ecumenical consideration of Scripture in two ways. First, as a method that does not begin with questions of historicity, this approach allows scholars of many persuasions to engage in discussion about the meaning of biblical stories without first being forced to reach agreement on any number of intractable historical issues.[10] For example, scholars may be able to discuss the literary meaning of a Bible story even if they do not agree on whether the events reported in the tale "really happened." In a sense, such unity is only superficial, brought on by a temporary suspension of discussion on questions that are in fact significant for all concerned. Still, there may be some value in representatives from different communities "agreeing to disagree" on certain matters and finding that they can cooperate and benefit from each other's insights on others.

An even greater potential for ecumenicity may lie in the recognition, on the part of some narrative critics, that a text can possess multiple meanings. Unlike some varieties of reader-response criticism, narrative criticism does hold that the text itself sets parameters for interpretation. Within these parameters, however, there may be some ambiguity; "gaps" in the text can make the exact response expected of the implied reader difficult to determine. When this happens, some narrative critics stress the need to nevertheless work toward the best possible interpretation of the text, that is, the interpretation most likely to be adopted by the implied reader as determined from what is provided. Other narrative critics, however, move in the direction of reader-response at this point and affirm ambiguity as the text's openness to be read in more ways than one. Such an attitude lays a foundation for more tolerant and accepting attitudes between believing communities who read texts with different interpretations.

7. *Narrative criticism offers fresh interpretations of biblical material.* This point follows from the just-mentioned fact that narrative criticism can allow for multiple interpretations of texts. Stories are often able to speak to people in ways that transcend the limitations of time and space. Some feminist and third-world theologians, for example, have discovered that narrative criticism opens the door for reading texts in a manner unfettered by what they regard as patriarchal or provincial restraints. Since the church needs continually to be reformed by scriptural challenges to the status quo, this aspect of narrative criticism is appealing. But narrative criticism is not the property of any particular special interest group. It is simply a methodology that enables the biblical stories to speak in ways that engage readers today.

8. *Narrative criticism unleashes the power of biblical stories for personal and social transformation.* There is increasing appreciation among scholars today for the ability of stories to engage us and to change the way we perceive ourselves and our world. What is it that makes stories so infectious? Some have suggested it is their resemblance to life itself; there is an intrinsic narrative quality underlying all human experience. Stories have the power to shape life because they formally embody "the shape of life."[11] This does not mean that stories derive their power from a referential function. Stories are not like life in many ways, and the most lifelike tales are not necessarily the ones that affect us most deeply. Rather, the narrative form itself corresponds in some profound way to reality and thus enables us to translate our experience of the story world into our own situation. Entering the story world of a narrative may be likened to attendance at a modern-day motion picture. Once inside the theater, we may find ourselves involved with a view of reality distinct from that of the world in which we actually live. Nevertheless it is possible for our encounter with this simplified and perhaps outlandish view of reality to have an effect on us, an effect that may continue to make itself felt long after we leave the theater and return to the real world.

Some advocates of narrative criticism have argued that this aspect of the methodology meets a need otherwise unaddressed by recent biblical scholarship. Culpepper has suggested that modern scholarship has tended to objectify the Gospels, forcing us to deal with them only on the rational level and thereby robbing the experience of interaction with the text of its native power.[12] Both historical investigation and doctrinal abstraction reify the biblical stories; they tear the message from its narrative context and force it into categories of thought that can never contain the distinctiveness, fascination, and authenticity of the stories themselves. Perhaps we need such order and objectivity, Culpepper concludes, but for most Christians the indispensable source of life and vitality for faith is neither a tentative historical reconstruction nor a statement of scripturally derived doctrinal principles. That source rather is the stories of the Bible themselves, remembered, treasured, and interpreted within their narrative form.[13]

For this discussion to degenerate into a debate over which should have primacy—the biblical stories or doctrinal abstraction concerning them—would be unfortunate. Both are important to the task of theology. Nevertheless, as generations of Bible readers can attest, something about the stories cannot be captured in any doctrinal formula. This is Culpepper's central point: By respecting the narrative character of biblical writings, narrative criticism adds a dimension to biblical studies that should be one essential component of the total theological enterprise.

Biblical literary criticism parallels other movements in systematic and practical theology that are also discovering or rediscovering the power of narrative. We hear of story theology, story preaching, and, in pastoral care, of a new emphasis on identifying one's personal story. A side benefit to using a story approach to the Bible at this time is that it provides opportunities for integration with these other disciplines.

OBJECTIONS TO NARRATIVE CRITICISM

In spite of the potential benefits that many believe narrative criticism has to offer, the method has not been introduced to biblical studies without controversy. A number of objections have been voiced concerning the legitimacy and advisability of using this approach for study of the Gospels.[14]

1. *Narrative criticism treats the Gospels as coherent narratives when they are actually collections of disparate material.* Drawing on the insights of form criticism, some scholars claim that it is wrong to classify the Gospels as "narratives" in the first place. For some form critics, the Gospels consisted of traditional units that had been strung together "like pearls on a string."[15] This juxtaposition of unrelated elements in a linear sequence created the "impression of a narrative," but such an illusion was accidental. Even before the advent of modern literary approaches, however, redaction critics discovered pervasive unifying features that can be found in each of the Gospels. Literary

studies have furthered such research and exposed a surprising coherence of narrative elements. For example, if the Gospel of Mark were merely a collection of diverse materials deriving from a variety of sources, one would not expect to find its principal character groups portrayed consistently throughout. Roland Mushat Frye, a scholar of literature, has examined our four Gospels and concluded that each of them appears to be "a narrative of considerable literary merit, in which diverse materials have been so effectively integrated that each Gospel should be treated as a literary work in its own right."[16]

Still, some say that narrative critics ignore or too easily dismiss inconsistencies in the Gospels. For example, the opening chapters of Luke's Gospel describe angels and spirit-filled prophets as proclaiming God's plan to restore Israel through Jesus, a plan that does not come to fruition in the later material. This can be explained through the recognition that Luke's "infancy narrative" belongs to a different source strata than the rest of the Gospel and, in some sense, must be considered independently. In its insistence on coherence, narrative criticism overlooks these "cracks and crevices" that occur in the Gospels as a result of the conflation of sources.[17]

This objection misses the point entirely, however, if it presumes that the legitimacy of narrative criticism depends upon establishing consistency at a content level. Narrative unity is not something that must be proved from an analysis of the material. Rather, it is something that can be assumed.[18] It is the form of narrative itself that grants coherence to the material, no matter how disparate that material might be. Accordingly, the so-called illusion of a narrative that was apparent even to the form critics is all that is required for this discipline. From the perspective of the implied reader, it will make no difference whether the narrative form was created accidentally or intentionally. It is there, and the reader must deal with it. The presence of inconsistencies in no way undermines the unity of a narrative but simply becomes one of the facets to be interpreted. They may, for instance, signal gaps and ambiguities that must be either explained or held in tension.[19] This is true regardless of whether they are there by design or negligence.

All works of literature have a compositional history, but the latter is not generally considered relevant for understanding the poetic function of the final product. From a historical perspective, it is certainly legitimate to try to determine where Chaucer found the stories incorporated in *Canterbury Tales*, but this information will not be determinative for the literary critic attempting to describe the effect of the finished work on its reader. Ultimately, then, this objection is ideological; the real question is whether the poetic function of the Gospels in the form that we now have them is a worthwhile subject for investigation. If it is, the somewhat complex processes that led to the Gospels' composition will not inhibit the undertaking of such research.

2. *Narrative criticism imposes on ancient literature concepts drawn from the study of modern literature.* Literary theory has without a doubt formulated most of its concepts in reference to modern literature. Bible students who explore secular textbooks on the subject find these works replete with references to Henry James, Jane Austen, Samuel Beckett, James Joyce, and so on. Is it not presumptuous to imagine that the biblical writers had the wherewithal to write with the finesse and subtlety ascribed to them through comparisons with modern authors?

This objection makes a valid point. It *is* important to recognize distinctions between modern and ancient literature, and narrative critics may sometimes fail to do so. Much in modern literary theory is not applicable to our Gospels. At the same time, some conventions of storytelling are timeless. Ancient stories, as well as modern ones, consist of events, characters, and settings and are told from a particular point of view. In fact, ancient literature often offers the best examples of basic storytelling technique precisely because the conventions are simple and are employed in a way that is not self-conscious. Failures or breakdowns with regard to the basic concepts of narrative criticism usually occur with regard to experimental modern literature rather than with regard to such archetypes of storytelling as are found in our Gospels.

It is not necessary to assume, furthermore, that the biblical writers had knowledge of literary concepts. The choice of narrative as a medium for their message committed them to certain basic conventions that can still be recognized and described today. John may not have known what "irony" meant. Still, from our perspective, his story frequently develops in ways that we would call ironic. To some extent, then, the terminology and categories of narrative criticism may be foreign impositions, but as long as this is remembered the substance of the analysis can be regarded as valid.

3. *Narrative criticism seeks to interpret the Gospels through methods that were devised for the study of fiction.* Many of the "narratologies" from which principles of narrative criticism are drawn are ostensibly intended to deal with fiction. Wayne Booth calls his book

The Rhetoric of Fiction. E. M. Forster's study is called *Aspects of the Novel.* Even Chatman's *Story and Discourse* bears the subtitle *Narrative Structure in Fiction and Film.* How can insights derived from the study of novels be applied directly to gospel research?

The Gospels are not works of fiction but intend to convey historical truth. To the extent that the genres of novel and gospel share a narrative form, however, both are subject to narrative analysis. We may recall Eric Auerbach's contention that "depictions of reality" are the subject of literary study; any narrative that presents such a depiction may be studied *as literature* regardless of whether or not the depiction is intended to be accepted as accurate.[20] The poetic function of any work that assumes a narrative form can be analyzed from the perspective of narrative criticism. Strictly speaking, the dichotomy between "history" and "fiction" in literature is a false one. It is better to speak of referential and poetic functions that can be attributed to all literature. The question is not whether the Gospels should be classed as history or as fiction, but whether they should be read in terms of their referential or poetic function. In reality, of course, they have always been read in both ways, but only recently has narrative criticism made the latter type of reading a subject of scholarly investigation and thereby conferred upon it a badge of academic respectability.

The fact that most secular narratology concentrates on novels simply reflects an unnecessary bias in the interests of that field. There is no reason why many of the principles found in *Story and Discourse* could not be applied to other genres than "fiction" and "film." Similar narrative structures are discernible in biographies and other nonfiction narrative works. In fact, narratologists do sometimes turn their attention to such literature as the works of Homer and the writings of Julius Caesar, although these represent quite different genres than that of the modern novel. Northrup Frye cites another famous example, Edward Gibbon's *Decline and Fall of the Roman Empire*, which was originally prized for its historical content, but has since come to be appreciated more for its quality as literature.[21]

In short, the form of the Gospels (as narratives) rather than their genre (as gospels) makes it possible to study them by employing narrative criticism. The recognition that they share certain formal characteristics with fictional works does not in any way prejudge the degree to which they reflect history or the reliability with which they do so.

4. *Narrative criticism lacks objective criteria for the analysis of texts.* It is sometimes said that literary-critical approaches endorse

subjective responses to texts and produce conclusions that are purely arbitrary. Christopher Tuckett connects this tendency with the proposition that a literary text can have multiple meanings and with the consequent rejection of authorial intention as determinate of a definitive "original meaning."[22] Historical-critical scholars may not always agree in their construal of original meaning, but at least they agree that the intention of the author is the criterion by which all proposals must be measured. Literary criticism, Tuckett contends, lacks any objective basis for evaluating interpretations. As an example, he suggests that a literary reading of Matthew's story of the sheep and goats (25:31-46) might interpret the parable as encouraging charitable giving to the poor and needy of the world. In fact, the original meaning of the story was more restricted, applying to responses made to Christian missionaries. Although the literary reading is certainly attractive, Tuckett wonders whether any scholarly integrity can be maintained when critics are free to read into texts meanings that were not intended.[23]

Tuckett's complaint is addressed to "literary criticism" in general, without further delineation of different approaches within that broad spectrum. There are some varieties of reader-oriented criticism that do encourage the sort of subjective reading that he finds objectionable. Narrative criticism, however, is a text-centered approach which holds that the text sets parameters on interpretation. I do not think a narrative critic would be likely to arrive at the "literary reading" for the story of the sheep and goats suggested by Tuckett, because such an interpretation would be ruled out by references within the text itself. Apart from any appeals to extratextual knowledge of early Christian communities, a narrative critic would note that the beneficiaries of charity in Matthew 25 are described as Jesus' "brothers." Elsewhere in Matthew's narrative, Jesus' brothers are defined as those who do the will of God (12:50). Accordingly, a narrative-critical reading of this passage may allow for a broader application than one circumscribed by relevance to first-century missionaries, but such a reading would not produce capricious applications that run counter to the context of the text itself.

To the extent that narrative criticism recognizes multiple meanings, the method can be viewed as embracing a degree of subjectivity. Narrative critics frequently disagree in their interpretation of texts and some (not all) narrative critics are willing to grant that, in some instances, more than one interpretion may be acceptable. The text sometimes allows itself to be read in more than one way. Narrative critics, however, place limits on this subjectivity. Even those who permit multiple interpretations recognize the "veto power" of the text with regard to interpretations that can *not* be maintained. Narrative criticism, then, does evaluate its interpretations according to objective criteria, but these criteria are defined in terms of the intention of *the text* rather than the intention of *the author.* The text, of course, includes what we have called the implied author and so takes into consideration authorial intent insofar as this has been incorporated into the text itself.

In one sense, the basis for interpretation adopted by narrative criticism is actually less conjectural than that accepted for traditional historical-critical investigation. The real authors of biblical books are not available for interview, so any reconstruction of their intention that goes beyond what can be found in the text is bound to be hypothetical. For narrative criticism, the standard for interpretation is the intention of the text, to which we have access today, rather than the supposed intentions of the authors, to which contemporary access is denied.

5. *Narrative criticism rejects or ignores the historical witness of the Gospels.* Probably the most pervasive objection to the use of narrative criticism in biblical studies is that the method is somehow antihistorical and so undermines the historical grounding of Christian faith. The Gospels are not treated as testimonies to God's action in history but are envisioned as having some intrinsic worth in and of themselves, apart from that of the events they describe. This conception, it is claimed, runs counter to the church's identification of these narratives as Scripture, which is based on an understanding that they are reliable records of salvation history rather than on an appreciation of their value as literature.

In reality, nothing in the assumptions or presuppositions of narrative criticism calls into question the legitimacy of historical investigation. There is no reason why a text that is examined with regard to its poetic function cannot also be examined by a different method that is interested in its referential function. The great majority of narrative critics discussed in this book are persons who do regard the historical witness of Scripture as important. Indeed, many of them have also used traditional methods of research to make significant contributions to our understanding and appreciation of this historical witness.[24]

Lynn Poland, in a recent critique of literary criticism, charges that its critical assumptions are "at odds with, or at least insufficient for, the full task of interpretation."[25] It is important to recognize, however, that the two indictments separated by Poland's "at least" are actually two very different matters. The charge that narrative criticism is at odds with the goals of historical interpretation cannot be maintained. Still, to the extent that narrative criticism is *non*historical (or, better, nonreferential), its results might be regarded as incomplete. But this objection merely indicates the limitations of the method without invalidating what contributions it does offer. One could argue that no one approach (source, form, redaction, etc.) is sufficient for the "full task of interpretation."

Even the perception that narrative criticism is "nonhistorical" must be mitigated. Narrative criticism demands that the modern reader have the historical information that the text assumes of its implied reader. Attention must be paid to what Iser calls "the reader's repertoire."[26] In a basic sense, this comprises practical information that is common knowledge in the world of the story: how much a denarius is worth, what a centurion does, and so forth. It may also include recognition of social and political realities that lie behind the story. It may involve understanding particular social customs and recognizing the meaning of culturally determined symbols or metaphors.[27] Narrative criticism must rely upon historical investigation to provide the reader with this sort of insight.

It is also possible for narrative criticism to make contributions to historical understanding. Kingsbury has suggested that the story world of the Gospels may well prove in important respects to be an "index" of the real world of the evangelist, and the implied reader may well prove to be an "index" of the real readers for whom the work was first intended.[28] I would add a third proposition (probably assumed by these two), namely, that the implied author may also serve as an index of the real author. For example, if the implied author of Mark's Gospel is sympathetic toward Jesus' disciples and regards them with optimism in spite of their failings, it is *likely* (though not certain) that the real author thought of them in this way also. Such an application of narrative-critical insights requires a hermeneutical leap, but it is a little one. Basically, the leap entails acceptance of the unprovable premise that the authors of our Gospels succeeded in creating narratives that would have the effects they wanted them to have. If these authors were successful, then the "intention of the text" discernible by narrative criticism can be regarded as a reliable index of the "intention of the author" sought by historical criticism. To the extent that scholars can make this "little leap," the results of narrative criticism will be useful in historical investigation. They will, at least, point historical scholarship in a particular direction that may subsequently be confirmed by other types of study.

In short, narrative criticism is certainly not an antihistorical discipline. In fact, a symbiotic relationship exists between narrative and historical approaches to texts. Although the two methods cannot be used simultaneously, they can be used side by side in a supplementary fashion. They might even be viewed as necessary complements, each providing information that is beneficial to the exercise of the other.

AN EXPANDED HERMENEUTIC

In biblical studies, the science of hermeneutics focuses on issues concerning the authority and inspiration of Scripture. Virtually all Christian communities are quick to identify the Bible as "the Word of God," even if there are different ideas as to how such an identification should be construed. At the very least, Christians believe that the Bible preserves a record of divine revelation that has been given at significant junctures in history. It contains testimonies of inspired persons and reports of God's actions that have abiding theological significance for us today.

An effective use of narrative criticism requires the development of a broader hermeneutic than this. The method assumes that revelation can also be an event that happens now, in a present encounter with the text. To be sure, the Bible is a record of how God spoke to people in the past, but it is also a channel through which God speaks to people today. Hermeneutical significance can be ascribed to the present act of reading (or hearing) the text.

To some, this conception may seem novel. But recipients are absolutely essential to any concept of revelation; without them, nothing can properly be said to have been revealed. According to the old adage, a tree that falls in a forest does not make a sound unless someone is there to hear it. Similarly, the Bible cannot be said to reveal God's Word unless someone receives this revelation. There is something almost blasphemous about calling a book that lies unopened on a coffee table, "the Word of God." According to Scripture itself, God's Word is an active, dynamic force that never returns void but accomplishes that for which it is sent (Isa. 55:11). The Word of God cleanses, heals, creates, judges, and saves, but it does not sit on coffee tables. A better formulation than saying, The Bible is the Word of God, would be to say, The Bible becomes the Word of God in those who receive it.[29]

98

Martin Luther regards the Word of God as first an event in history, then as the proclamation of that event by the biblical writers, and finally as the event in which that proclamation elicits and enacts faith in those who hear it.[30] Even scholars who pay homage to Luther's hermeneutic, however, often ignore the significance of his final stage. Traditional methods of biblical interpretation have recognized the importance of the historical past as a locus for revelation and have succeeded in enlightening us with regard to the historical circumstances to which the texts attest and with regard to the conditions that led to their production. Very little attention, however, has been paid to the interpretive processes through which these texts are appropriated in the present. Narrative criticism attempts to fill this gap in biblical studies by examining the ways in which texts become meaningful to readers. The use of this method is hermeneutically significant for the church in that it enables scholars to complete the full task of interpretation in a way that does not limit revelation to events that happened in the past.

Any hermeneutic that locates revelation primarily in the past is inevitably pessimistic. The very passing of time, which is definitive of history, distances us from the significant event and places us at an ever-greater disadvantage. The sentiment that accompanies such a perspective is the suspicion that we are missing something: if only we had been there, we would understand better. The hermeneutic that undergirds narrative criticism challenges this prejudice. Revelation is given through the story, which remains with us today. We are, in fact, in a privileged position, for the story interprets the events for us in ways that we might never have grasped if we had simply been there to witness them transpire in history.

Narrative criticism also counters a reductive tendency to equate truth with history. Biblical scholars have always recognized that "truth requires a larger field than history."[31] Within the Bible, truth is conveyed through a diversity of forms, including psalms, prayers, parables, and proverbs. Still, as Hans Frei notes, the "history-like" character of the Gospels has often seduced scholars into believing that these books convey truth only insofar as they are historically accurate.[32] Narrative criticism corrects this assumption. Whatever value may be assigned to the historical witness of the Gospels, these books may also be read as "true stories," that is, as stories intended to evoke responses that are in keeping with the true will of God.

99

If God is able to speak through story as well as through history, then the poetic witness of these narratives is no less significant for us today than their referential witness. Both types of testimony, furthermore, presuppose interpretive chasms that must be crossed. Scholars who have studied Scripture with a primary interest in its referential function have long recognized the existence of such a gap between "the meaning then" and "the meaning now."[33] The goal of historical-critical study has been to elucidate the meaning that a particular text is thought to have had at a given stage in its composition. After this goal is accomplished, however, most contemporary Christians will want to determine the relevance of this historically conditioned meaning for their present situation. It is beyond the capacity of historical-critical scholarship to make such a translation. In order to derive "the meaning now" from the critically determined "meaning then," the interpreter must rely on the gift of the Spirit and on insights drawn from other fields, such as systematic theology and pastoral care.

Scholars who use narrative criticism to bring out the poetic meaning of a text encounter a chasm of a different kind. This time, it is a gulf between the story world of the narrative and the real world of the reader. Even when a reader has come to understand what a story "means," the significance of that story's meaning for real life remains to be determined. The real world is never identical with the world of a story, even if that story is regarded as portraying life in the real world quite accurately. For example, people in real life are generally less predictable than the flat characters we encounter in our Gospel narratives. Relationships are more complex and options more numerous. There is no reliable, omniscient narrator providing us with all the data we need to make sense of our surroundings. For these reasons, the meaning of a biblical story as elucidated through narrative criticism does not translate immediately into meaning for real life. Once again, the full task of biblical interpretation requires gifts and insights that are not provided by the exegetical discipline itself.

The popularity and success of literary approaches to the Bible has led some scholars to suggest that critical scholarship is in the midst of "a paradigm shift," similar to the earlier revolution in which dogmatic interpretation was replaced by historical-critical methodology.[34] Even staunch supporters of the historical-critical method have been led to question whether it will continue to be practiced.[35] It seems unlikely, however, that Christians will ever be satisfied with simply reading their stories of faith as stories, without wanting to inquire into the history

100

behind them. As people of faith, we are not just interested in the meaning of these stories, but also in the "significance of their meaning."[36] If the story of Jesus' passion, for instance, was simply an imaginative tale with no basis in history, it would still be very meaningful. The significance, however, of this "meaningful story" would not be the same. It might serve as an illustrative example of sacrificial love, but it could hardly provide the basis for a doctrine of substitutionary atonement. Narrative criticism, then, can only serve theology so far. It can determine the meaning of stories, but not, ultimately, the significance of their meaning.[37]

Another limitation can also be noted. Because narrative criticism attempts to understand each Gospel on its own terms, the interpreter will finally be left with four different stories of Jesus. But how are these to be related? Is it possible to speak of a "story of Jesus," in the singular?[38] While narrative criticism can call attention to the distinctive effects produced by each of the Gospels, the synthesizing of these for biblical theology as a whole will no doubt require contributions from other quarters.

Different methodological approaches to exegetical study may be likened to a set of keys on a ring.[39] The various keys open different doors and grant access to different types of insight. Narrative criticism has been able to open some doors that had previously been closed to scholars. It provides answers to questions that people of faith ask about the Bible and about the meaning of biblical material. But it will not open all the doors. Some questions that may be very important to people of faith narrative criticism cannot answer. Some of these may yield to a historical-critical inquiry; others require assistance from outside the field of biblical sciences altogether. Thus, the wise scribe Jesus speaks of in Matt. 13:52 treasures both what is new and what is old. Likewise, in days to come, the wise interpreter of the Bible will want to have as full a set of keys as possible.

Appendix:
Using Narrative Criticism
in Exegesis

Narrative criticism focuses on understanding the Gospels as entire books. In practical terms, however, exegesis that serves the teaching and preaching ministry of the church is usually expected to elucidate single texts or pericopes. Such an interpretation of "episodes" can be accomplished from the perspective of narrative criticism by asking the sorts of questions that are presented here. Of course, not all questions will apply equally to all texts.

Events

1. What is the event that transpires in this episode? What "happens" in this passage?

2. How important is this event when compared with other events in the story? Does it represent a major turning point in the narrative or is it simply a logical outworking of something that has happened already? See above, pp. 36, 44–45.

3. How is the event reported in terms of narrative time? Is it out of sequence? Is it told with either a noticeable economy or abundance of detail? Is it an event that happens repeatedly, or are there other references to this event elsewhere in the narrative? See above, pp. 36–39, 45.

4. How is this event related to other events in the narrative? Has its occurrence been made possible, likely, or even necessary by something else that has happened? Does it in turn make the occurrence of other events more possible, likely, or necessary? See above, pp. 40–42, 45–46.

5. What elements of conflict are discernible here? How does the nature and intensity of conflict in this passage compare with what is

103

found elsewhere in the narrative? How is the conflict found here eventually resolved? Does this event contribute in any significant way to the development and ultimate resolution of this conflict? See above, pp. 42–44, 46–48.

6. What conclusions can be drawn about the role this event plays in the overall story? What does the event contribute to the plot as a whole?

Characters

1. Who are the characters in this episode and do they appear elsewhere in the narrative? Are any of these characters actually representative of a character group that fulfills a single role in the story? See above, pp. 51, 58.

2. How are the characters in this passage revealed to the reader? Does the narrator tell us about them? Do we learn about them through reports of their actions, speech, thoughts, or beliefs? Or do we learn about them through reports of other characters' actions, speech, thoughts, or beliefs concerning them? Is this consistent with the way we learn about these same characters elsewhere in the narrative? See above, pp. 52–53, 58–59.

3. What is the evaluative point of view espoused by each of the characters in this episode? Are the characters oriented toward truth or untruth? Is this consistent with their characterization elsewhere in the narrative? See above, pp. 53–54, 60–61.

4. What traits are ascribed to each of the characters in this episode? Do these traits derive from some root trait, or do they perhaps serve as root traits that lead to other qualities? Are the traits that can be recognized here consistent with those attributed to these characters elsewhere in the narrative? Are the characters better described as round, flat, or stock characters in the narrative as a whole? See above, pp. 54–55, 61–64.

5. Is the reader likely to empathize either idealistically or realistically with any of these characters? Can the attitude of either the narrator or the protagonist toward the characters be determined? Will the reader regard the characters with sympathy or antipathy? See above, pp. 56–58, 64–65.

Settings

1. What are the spatial, temporal, and social settings for this episode and how do they contribute to the mood of the narrative? Are

these same settings found elsewhere in the narrative or are they unique to this particular passage?

2. With regard to spatial settings, how does the physical environment of the characters in this episode affect their actions? Through what sensory data are the physical surroundings described and is this type of description typical for the narrative? Do any of the physical features have symbolic connotations either here or elsewhere in the narrative? Can relevant oppositions (e.g., "inside" versus "outside") be discerned with regard to any of these settings or do the settings provide boundaries between such oppositions? See above, pp. 70–72, 75–78.

3. With regard to temporal settings, what sort of chronological and typological references are used in this episode? What connotations are associated in this narrative with the "kind of time" (e.g., day or night, winter or summer) within which this episode transpires? Finally, how can what happens here be interpreted in light of the narrative's concept of time in general (that is, "monumental time" or salvation history)? See above, pp. 72–74, 78–82.

4. With regard to social settings, what is the cultural context for what transpires in this episode? What knowledge is the reader assumed to possess concerning political institutions, class structures, economic systems, social customs, and the like? How does this information affect the interpretation of this particular episode within the context of the narrative as a whole? See above, pp. 74–75, 82–83.

Overall Interpretation

1. What rhetorical devices are employed in the reporting of this episode? Can intentional symbolism or irony be detected? What narrative patterns are used in structuring this passage and its immediate context? See above, pp. 23–34.

2. What does this episode, as understood within the context of the entire narrative, reveal about the implied author? What values, ideas, priorities, or preferences seem to govern the way in which this story is told? See above, pp. 5–6.

3. What effect does the narrative seem to assume that this episode will have upon its readers? What elements of the narrative's discourse contribute to the production of this effect?

Abbreviations

AARAS	American Academy of Religion Academy **Series**
BALS	Bible and Literature Series
BiblRes	*Biblical Research*
CBQ	*Catholic Biblical Quarterly*
CritInq	*Critical Inquiry*
GBS	Guides to Biblical Scholarship
IDB	*Interpreter's Dictionary of the Bible*
Int	*Interpretation*
JAAR	*Journal of the American Academy of Religion*
JAMA	*Journal of the American Medical Association*
JBL	*Journal of Biblical Literature*
JSNT	*Journal for the Study of the New Testament*
JSNTSS	Journal for the Study of the New Testament Supplement Series
JSOTSS	Journal for the Study of the Old Testament Supplement Series
NLH	*New Literary History*
NTS	*New Testament Studies*
PAW	*Princeton Alumni Weekly*
PhilRhet	*Philosophy and Rhetoric*
PTMS	Pittsburgh Theological Monograph Series
RevExp	*Review and Expositor*
SBL	Society of Biblical Literature
SBLDS	Society of Biblical Literature Dissertation Series
TI	Theological Inquiries
TSR	*Trinity Seminary Review*
USQR	*Union Seminary Quarterly Review*

Notes

Chapter 1: Scripture as Story

1. For what follows, see also Mark Allan Powell, "The Bible and Modern Literary Criticism," in Betty A. O'Brien, *Summary of Proceedings: Forty-third Annual Conference of the American Libraries Association* (St. Meinrad, Ind.: ATLA, 1990), 78–94.

2. See Edgar McKnight, *The Bible and the Reader: An Introduction to Literary Criticism* (Philadelphia: Fortress Press, 1985); Norman R. Petersen, "Literary Criticism in Biblical Studies," in Richard Spencer, *Orientation by Disorientation. Studies in Literary Criticism and Biblical Literary Criticism Presented in Honor of William A. Beardslee*, PTMS 35 (Pittsburgh: Pickwick Press, 1955), 25–50.

3. See Edgar Krentz, *The Historical-Critical Method*, GBS (Philadelphia: Fortress Press, 1975).

4. See Hans W. Frei, *The Eclipse of Biblical Narrative: A Study in Eighteenth and Nineteenth Century Hermeneutics* (New Haven, Conn.: Yale University Press, 1974).

5. William A. Beardslee, *Literary Criticism of the New Testament*, GBS (Philadelphia: Fortress Press, 1969).

6. Funk, *Language, Hermeneutic, and the Word of God* (New York: Harper & Row, 1966); Via, *The Parables: Their Literary and Existential Dimension* (Philadelphia: Fortress Press, 1967); Crossan, *In Parables* (New York: Harper & Row, 1973).

7. Norman Perrin, "The Evangelist As Author: Reflections on Method in the Study and Interpretation of the Synoptic Gospels and Acts," *BiblRes* 17 (1972): 5–18, esp. 9–10.

8. Norman R. Petersen, *Literary Criticism for New Testament Critics*, GBS (Philadelphia: Fortress Press, 1978), 20.

9. Beardslee, *Literary Criticism*, 3.

10. Rene Welleck and Austin Warren, *Theory of Literature*, 3d ed. (San Diego: Harcourt, Brace, Jovanovich, 1975), 20–28.

11. Erich Auerbach, *Mimesis: The Representation of Reality in Western Literature*, trans. W. Trask (Garden City, N.Y.: Doubleday and Co., 1957; German ed.).

12. See Meyer Howard Abrams, *A Glossary of Literary Terms*, 4th ed. (New York: Holt, Rinehart, and Winston, 1981), 117–19.

13. S. Bermann, "Revolution in Literary Criticism," *PAW* (Nov. 21, 1984): 10. Cited by Tremper Longman, *Literary Approaches to Biblical Interpretation* (Grand Rapids, Mich.: Zondervan, 1987), 19.

14. Abrams, *Glossary*, 83.

15. Even E. D. Hirsch admits that authors mean more than they are aware of meaning. See *Validity in Interpretation* (New Haven, Conn.: Yale University Press, 1967), 48, 51, 61, and his expanded view in *The Aims of Interpretation* (Chicago: University of Chicago Press, 1976), 74–92.

16. See Wayne Booth, *The Rhetoric of Fiction*, 2d ed. (Chicago: University of Chicago Press, 1983), 66–77; Seymour Chatman, *Story and Discourse: Narrative Structure in Fiction and Film* (Ithaca, N.Y.: Cornell University Press, 1978), 147–51; and the items listed in Booth's bibliography, 478–80, 511–12.

17. Even Luke and Acts are usually read as two parts of a single work rather than as two separate books by the same author.

18. A narrative will have a single implied author even though it "may have been composed by a committee (Hollywood films) or by a disparate group of people over a long period of time (many folk ballads)" (so Chatman, *Story and Discourse*, 140).

19. Exceptions include Northrup Frye, *The Great Code: The Bible and Literature* (New York: Harcourt, Brace, Jovanovich, 1982), and Frank Kermode, *The Genesis of Secrecy: On The Interpretation of Narrative* (Cambridge: Harvard Unviversity Press, 1979).

20. David Rhoads and Donald Michie, *Mark As Story: An Introduction to the Narrative of a Gospel* (Philadelphia: Fortress Press, 1982).

21. Prior to this book, the most comprehensive such study had been an unpublished dissertation by Thomas E. Boomershine, "Mark the Storyteller: A Rhetorical-Critical Investigation of Mark's Passion and Resurrection Narrative" (Union Theological Seminary, New York, 1974). Werner Kelber's *Mark's Story of Jesus* (Philadelphia: Fortress Press, 1979) was also insightful, but was more heavily influenced by traditional historical concerns.

22. Jack Dean Kingsbury, *The Christology of Mark's Gospel* (Philadelphia: Fortress Press, 1983).

23. R. Alan Culpepper, *Anatomy of the Fourth Gospel: A Study in Literary Design* (Philadelphia: Fortress Press, 1983).

24. Rhoads, "Narrative Criticism and the Gospel of Mark," *JAAR* 50 (1982): 411–34. This paper was originally delivered in 1980 at the 10th and final year of the SBL Seminar on Mark. Much of the work that led to the development of narrative criticism was undertaken in this seminar, which was chaired first by Norman Perrin, and then by Werner Kelber. Rhoads cites Thomas Boomershine, Joanna Dewey, Robert Fowler, Norman Petersen, Robert Tannehill, and Mary Ann Tolbert as seminar members who were particularly influential in the development of the new discipline.

110

25. Jack Dean Kingsbury, *Matthew As Story* (Philadelphia: Fortress Press, 1986); Robert Tannehill, *The Narrative Unity of Luke-Acts: A Literary Interpretation*, 2 vols. (Philadelphia and Minneapolis: Fortress Press, 1986 and 1990).

26. A fifth scholar, Norman R. Petersen, must also be mentioned. His essays, "Point of View in Mark's Narrative," *Semeia* 12 (1978): 97–121, and "Story Time and Plotted Time in Mark's Gospel" (chapter 3 of *Literary Criticism for New Testament Critics*) were enormously influential. Although he has never contributed a full-length study of an entire narrative book, Petersen has in many ways served as this movement's premier theorist.

27. Here and elsewhere in this book, I am focusing on varieties of literary criticism that have been especially significant for recent developments in biblical studies. Stephen Moore may be correct that the "impression being fostered among biblical scholars that secular literary criticism is a discipline preoccupied with the unity of texts and the autonomy of story worlds" is actually "well wide of the mark—except in the sense that these have been among the concepts most contested in recent years" (See Moore, *Literary Criticism and the Gospels: The Theoretical Challenge* (New Haven, Conn.: Yale University Press, 1989), 11. Discussion of the full range of literary theories is beyond the scope of this book.

28. This is also true of what has been called *canonical criticism*, though in other ways the latter approach retains typical historical concerns. See Brevard S. Childs, *The New Testament As Canon: An Introduction* (Philadelphia: Fortress Press, 1988); James A. Sanders, *Canon and Community: A Guide to Canonical Criticism*, GBS (Philadelphia: Fortress Press, 1984).

29. One aspect of redaction criticism, called *composition analysis*, does examine the manner in which units of tradition have been ordered and arranged in the work as a whole. Still, the concern is with unity of theological perspective rather than with unity of story. See Moore, *Literary Criticism*, 4–7.

30. Murray Krieger, *A Window to Criticism: Shakespeare's Sonnets and Modern Poetics* (Princeton: Princeton University Press, 1964), 3.

31. Also influential is John Austin's *How To Do Things With Words*, 2d ed., (Cambridge: Harvard University Press, 1975). See Abrams, *Glossary*, 181–83; Chatman, *Story and Discourse*, 161–66; Hugh C. White, ed. *Speech Act Theory and Biblical Criticism. Semeia* 41 (1988).

32. Petersen, *Literary Criticism for New Testament Critics*, 11–20.

33. Ibid., 24–48; see also Paul Hernadi, "Literary Theory: A Compass for Critics," *CritInq* 3 (1976): 369–86.

Chapter 2: Ways of Reading

1. See Abrams, *Glossary*.

2. Abrams, *The Mirror and the Lamp: Romantic Theory and the Critical Tradition* (New York: W. W. Norton, 1958), 8–29.

3. For a comparative analysis of these movements, see also Mark Allan Powell, "Types of Readers and Their Relevance for Biblical Hermeneutics," *TSR* 12 (1990).

4. See Daniel Patte, *Structural Exegesis for New Testament Critics*, GBS (Minneapolis: Fortress Press, 1989).

5. Propp, *Morphology of the Folktale*, trans. L. Scott, 2d ed. (Austin: University of Texas, 1968; Russian ed. 1928).

6. Patte, *The Gospel According to Matthew: A Structural Commentary on Matthew's Faith* (Philadelphia: Fortress Press, 1987).

7. See George Kennedy, *New Testament Interpretation Through Rhetorical Criticism* (Chapel Hill: University of North Carolina Press, 1984); Burton Mack, *Rhetoric and the New Testament*, GBS (Minneapolis: Fortress Press, 1989).

8. *Art of Poetry*.

9. *Orator* 69.

10. *The "Art" of Rhetoric*, 3.1.1358a. See also *The Poetics*.

11. Lloyd Bitzer, "The Rhetorical Situation," *PhilRhet* 1 (1968): 1–14, esp. 5–6.

12. Rhetorical criticism differs, however, from reader-response approaches described elsewhere in this chapter. Whereas rhetorical criticism attempts to understand the text from the perspective of its original intended readers, reader-response approaches seek to understand the effect of the text on modern readers.

13. Two attempts have been made to investigate the Gospel of Mark as a whole literary unit from a rhetorical point of view. See Burton Mack, *A Myth of Innocence: Mark and Christian Origins* (Philadelphia: Fortress Press, 1988); Vernon K. Robbins, *Jesus the Teacher. A Socio-rhetorical Interpretation of Mark* (Philadelphia: Fortress Press, 1984).

14. Betz, *Galatians: A Commentary on Paul's Letter to the Churches in Galatia*, Hermeneia (Philadelphia: Fortress Press, 1979).

15. Kennedy, *New Testament Interpretation*, 39–85, 97–113.

16. See Robert Detweiler, ed., *Reader-Response Approaches to Biblical and Secular Texts. Semeia* 31 (1985); Robert M. Fowler, *Let the Reader Understand: Reader-Response Criticism and the Gospel of Mark* (Bloomington: Indiana University Press, 1989); McKnight, *Bible and the Reader*, 75–134; idem, *Post-Modern Use of the Bible: The Emergence of Reader-Oriented Criticism* (Nashville: Abingdon Press, 1988); James Resseguie, "Reader-Response and the Synoptic Gospels," *JAAR* (1982): 411–34.

17. Robert Scholes and Robert Kellogg, *The Nature of Narrative* (New York: Oxford University Press, 1966), 4.

18. Its organization owes much to Resseguie, "Reader-Response and the Synoptic Gospels," and to Susan Suleimann, "Varieties of Audience-Oriented Criticism," in S. Suleimann and I. Crossman, *The Reader in the Text: Essays on Audience and Interpretation* (Princeton: Princeton University Press, 1980), 3–21. The former identifies the three broad categories marked here by Roman numerals; the latter identifies six types of reader-response criticism: rhetorical, structuralist, phenomenological, psychoanalytic, sociological, and hermeneutic.

19. Cf. John Dominic Crossan, ed., *Derrida and Biblical Studies, Semeia* 23 (1982).

20. Longman, *Literary Approaches*, 41.

21. Holland, *The Dynamics of Literary Response* (New York: W. W. Norton, 1968); idem, *Five Readers Reading* (New Haven, Conn.: Yale University Press, 1975); "A Transactive Account of Transactive Criticism," *Poetics* 7 (1978): 177–89. Other literary theories employing psychoanalytic concepts have been advanced by David Bleich and Harold Bloom. See Bleich, *Subjective Criticism* (Baltimore: John Hopkins University Press, 1978); Bloom, *Kabbalah and Criticism* (New York: Continuum, 1983).

22. Fish, *Is There a Text in This Class? The Authority of Interpretive Communities* (Cambridge: Harvard University Press, 1980). In spite of Fish's structuralist affinities, I regard his view as fitting the "reader over the text" paradigm, because he defines interpretive communities as preexistent to critical consensus.

23. Fish, "Literature in the Reader: Affective Stylistics," in *Self-Consuming Artifacts*, (Berkeley and Los Angeles: University of California Press, 1972), 383–427. Fish later decided that affective stylistics represents only one strategy that an interpretive community might choose to use; it is in executing such a choice that dominance *over* the text becomes apparent.

24. See Wolfgang Iser, *The Act of Reading: A Theory of Aesthetic Response* (Baltimore: Johns Hopkins University Press, 1978); idem, *The Implied Reader: Patterns of Communication in Prose Fiction from Bunyan to Beckett* (Baltimore: Johns Hopkins University Press, 1974).

25. Cf. Jack D. Kingsbury, "Reflections on 'the Reader' of Matthew's Gospel," *NTS* 34 (1988): 442–60; Robert M. Fowler, "Who is 'the Reader' in Reader-Response Criticism?" *Semeia* 31 (1985): 5–23.

26. Chatman, *Story and Discourse*, 149–50.

27. Kingsbury, *Matthew As Story*, 38.

28. Reading in this manner requires what Coleridge called "a willful suspension of disbelief." Similarly, Paul Ricoeur speaks of "the adoption of a second naivete." See *The Symbolism of Evil*, trans. E. Buchanan (New York: Harper & Row, 1967), 351.

29. Compare Kingsbury's *Matthew As Story* with Richard Edwards, *Matthew's Story of Jesus* (Philadelphia: Fortress Press, 1985). A key difference is that Edwards assumes a first-time reader.

30. See the afterword to the second edition of Booth's *Rhetoric of Fiction*, esp. 421–31, and the interview with Iser conducted by Booth and Norman Holland in *Diacritics* 10 (1980): 57–74.

Chapter 3: Story and Discourse

1. Norman R. Petersen suggests that Paul's letters may be subject to literary analysis insofar as there are stories behind the letters. See *Rediscovering Paul: Philemon and the Sociology of Paul's Narrative World* (Philadelphia: Fortress Press, 1985).

2. Chatman, *Story and Discourse*, 15–42.

3. Ibid., 3.

4. Jack D. Kingsbury, "The Figure of Jesus in Matthew's Story: A Literary-Critical Probe," *JSNT* 21 (1984): 3–36, esp. 4–7. Cf. *Matthew As Story*, 34, n. 118.

5. This does not necessarily mean that Satan's point of view is always incorrect. Demons, for instance, correctly identify Jesus as the Son of God (Mark 1:24; 3:11; 5:7), but they are wrong to do so, and their attitude toward Jesus as Son of God is also wrong. The concept of evaluative point of view assumes a wider notion of truth than simple accuracy.

6. Cf. Petersen, "Point of View in Mark's Narrative."

7. Booth, *Rhetoric of Fiction*, 3–4.

8. Note, for instance, the oft-repeated comments by the narrator of the Deuteronomistic History to the effect that someone "did what was evil in the sight of the Lord" or "did what was right in the eyes of the Lord." Even Luke 1:6 is less presumptuous.

9. For example, John 3, where it is impossible to tell when the words of Jesus leave off and the words of the narrator begin. See Culpepper, *Anatomy of Fourth Gospel*, 34–43.

10. James Dawsey has suggested that Luke does employ a narrator who proves unreliable. See *The Lukan Voice. Confusion and Irony in the Gospel of Luke* (Macon, Ga.: Mercer University Press, 1988). His thesis has been discounted by other narrative critics (Tannehill, *Narrative Unity* vol. 1, p. 7, n. 4).

11. The distinction between implied author and narrator becomes less critical when the latter is regarded as reliable, but some differentiation may still be made. For example, the reader of Mark's Gospel may accept the near omniscience of the narrator without imagining that the implied author is omniscient as well.

12. William D. Edwards, Wesley J. Gabel, and Floyd E. Hosmer, "On the Physical Death of Jesus Christ," *JAMA* 255 (1986): 1455–63, esp. 1456. Cf. Roland Mushat Frye, "Language for God and Feminist Language: A Literary and Rhetorical Analysis," *Int* 43 (1989): 45–57, esp. 56.

13. Culpepper, *Anatomy of Fourth Gospel*, 165.

14. Ibid., 181.

15. *Metaphor and Reality*, (Bloomington: Indiana University Press, 1962), 99–110.

16. John Darr, " 'This Fox': A Literary Interpretation of Jesus' Epithet for Herod in Luke 13:32," unpublished paper presented at 1988 SBL annual meeting, Synoptic Gospels Section.

17. Boris Uspensky, *A Poetics of Composition: The Structure of the Artistic Text and Typology of a Compositional Form* (Berkeley and Los Angeles: University of California Press, 1973).

18. Scholes and Kellogg, *Nature of Narrative*, 240.

19. D. C. Mueke, *The Compass of Irony* (London: Methuen, 1969), 19–20.

20. This is true of what he calls "stable irony." See *A Rhetoric of Irony* (Chicago: University of Chicago Press, 1974), 5–6.

21. Paul Duke, *Irony in the Fourth Gospel* (Atlanta: John Knox Press, 1985), 2.

22. Cf. Culpepper, *Anatomy of Fourth Gospel*, 169–75.

23. Cf. Rhoads and Michie, *Mark As Story*, 60.

24. For a full discussion of such clues, see Wayne Booth, *A Rhetoric of Irony* (Chicago: University of Chicago Press, 1974), 47–90.

25. Ibid., 10–13. Booth details these four steps with regard to the perception of verbal irony. In the case of symbolism or of situational irony, the first step might entail rejection of an *exclusively* literal meaning.

26. Ibid., 12.

27. Chatman, *Story and Discourse*, 229.

28. Duke, *Irony in Fourth Gospel*, 38–39.

29. Culpepper, *Anatomy of Fourth Gospel*, 151.

30. See David Bauer, *The Structure of Matthew's Gospel: A Study in Literary Design*, JSNTSS 31/BALS 15 (Sheffield: Almond Press, 1988), 13–20. Cf. Robert Traina, *Methodical Bible Study: A New Approach to Hermeneutics* (Grand Rapids, Mich.: Zondervan, 1985; originally published in 1952), 50–59; Howard Kuist, *How To Enjoy the Bible* (Richmond: John Knox Press, 1939); idem, *These Words Upon Thy Heart: Scripture and the Christian Response* (Richmond: John Knox Press, 1947), 80–87, 159–81.

31. Rhoads and Michie, *Mark As Story*, 47–49. They call the devise a "two-step progression."

32. See the analysis of "concentric patterns" in Joanna Dewey, "The Literary Structure of the Controversy Stories in Mark 2:1—3:6," *JBL* 92 (1973): 394–401. Cf. Rhoads and Michie, *Mark As Story*, 51–54.

33. Bauer, *Structure of Matthew*, 19–20.

Chapter 4: Events

1. Chatman, *Story and Discourse*, 43–44.

2. Ibid., 45.

3. I present Barthes as interpreted by Chatman (*Story and Discourse*, 53–56). The terms kernel and satellite are Chatman's translation of Barthes' *noyau* and *catalyse*.

4. Chatman, *Story and Discourse*, 55–56.

5. Gerard Genette, *Narrative Discourse: An Essay in Method* (Ithaca, N.Y.: Cornell University Press, 1975).

6. For further distinctions, see Genette, *Narrative Discourse*, 33–85; Culpepper, *Anatomy of Fourth Gospel*, 54–70; and Robert W. Funk, *The Poetics of Biblical Narrative* (Sonoma, Calif.: Polebridge Press, 1988), 187–206.

7. To use the more traditional terminology of salvation history, Matthew views the time of Jesus (earthly and exalted) as a new era of "fulfillment," distinct from the old age of "promise." See Kingsbury, *Matthew: Structure, Christology, Kingdom* (Minneapolis: Fortress Press, 1989; originally published 1975), 25–36.

8. Genette, *Narrative Discourse*, 86–112. Cf. Chatman, *Story and Discourse*, 67–78.

9. Genette, *Narrative Discourse*, 113–60. Cf. Chatman, *Story and Discourse*, 78–79.

10. Edward Morgan Forster, *Aspects of the Novel* (New York: Harcourt, Brace, Jovanovich, 1927), 86.

11. Chatman, *Story and Discourse*, 45–46.

12. The question of whether readers should be expected to infer such causes when they are not at least implicitly indicated is also discussed by Gerald Prince and Shlomith Rimmon-Kenan. For a good summary, see Funk, *Poetics*, 52–58.

13. Note the difference in the way this term is used here and the way it is used by Aristotle. The latter describes episodic plots as ones "in which the episodes do not follow each other probably or inevitably" (*Poetics* 9,9).

14. Paul Goodman has offered a much-quoted description of such literature: "In the beginning anything is possible; in the middle things become probable; and in the ending everything is necessary." See *The Structure of Literature*, (Chicago: University of Chicago Press, 1954), 14.

15. Chatman, *Story and Discourse*, 45.

16. Laurence Perrine, *Story and Structure*, 4th ed. (New York: Harcourt, Brace, Jovonovich, 1974), 44.

17. Ibid.

18. Cf. Kingsbury, *Matthew As Story*, 73.

19. Cf. Norman R. Petersen, "When Is the End Not the End? Literary Reflections on the Ending of Mark's Narrative," *Int* 34 (1980): 151–66.

20. For a fuller treatment of this subject, see my article "The Plot and Subplots of Matthew's Gospel," to be published in *NTS*. Also see Bauer, *Structure of Matthew's Gospel*; Edwards, *Matthew's Story of Jesus*; Kingsbury, *Matthew As Story*; Frank Matera, "The Plot of Matthew's Gospel," *CBQ* 49 (1987): 233–53; Dan Via, "Structure, Christology and Ethics in Matthew," in Spencer, *Orientation By Disorientation*, 199–216.

21. Matera, "Plot of Matthew's Gospel," 243–46.

22. These are usually called the Sermon on the Mount (Matt. 5–7), the missionary discourse (9:35—10:42), the parable discourse (13:1—52), the community discourse (17:24—18:35), and the eschatological discourse (Matt. 24–25).

23. Bauer, *Structure of Matthew's Gospel*, 73–108.

24. Insofar as Jesus has also come "to call sinners" (9:13), he fulfills the goal of saving people from sin to some extent through his earthly life and ministry. In Matthew's narrative, however, that goal is ultimately fulfilled only through Jesus' death on the cross.

25. I am only in partial agreement, then, with Matera's view. Although the great commission does inaugurate "a new beginning," the "climax of the entire Gospel" is Jesus' death on the cross. See Ronald Witherup, "The Cross of Jesus: A Literary-Critical Study of Matthew 27," Ph.D. diss., Union Theological Seminary in Virginia, 1985.

26. No one has done more to demonstrate the essential christological character of Matthew than Kingsbury. A victim of his own success, he has established some of his points so securely that they now appear self-evident.

27. Kingsbury prefers to speak of "story lines," which can be traced with regard to each of the major characters. See *Matthew As Story*.

28. For an extended treatment of Matt. 27:55—28:20, see Keith Howard Reeves, "The Resurrection Narrative in Matthew: A Literary-Critical Examination," Ph.D. diss., Union Theological Seminary in Virginia, 1988.

29. Bauer, *Structure of Matthew's Gospel*, 129–34; Kingsbury, *Matthew As Story*, 105–14.

30. Space does not permit discussion here of a completely different approach to plot that is sometimes taken. The plot of a narrative can be analyzed according to the vicissitudes of its protagonist. Chatman (*Story and Discourse*, 84–95) lists several taxonomies that have been developed for classifying plots as "comedies," "tragedies," "romances," and the like. He regards such typologies, however, as "highly questionable," and this approach has not yet been applied with much enthusiasm in narrative criticism of the Gospels. Cf. Culpepper, *Anatomy of Fourth Gospel*, 80–84.

Chapter 5: Characters

1. Cf. Perrine, *Story and Structure*, 67.

2. Henry James, "The Art of Fiction," in *Partial Portraits* (London: MacMillan, 1888).

3. Chatman, *Story and Discourse*, 116–26.

4. Booth, *Rhetoric of Fiction*, 3–20.

5. Uspensky, *Poetics of Composition*, 8–100.

6. Ibid., 8.

7. Petersen, "Point of View in Mark's Narrative." Cf. J. M. Lotman, "Point of View in a Text," *NLH* 6 (1975): 339–52, esp. 343.

8. Chatman, *Story and Discourse*, 121. See also the definitions of Gordon W. Allport in this same section.

9. Lack of love for God is explicitly ascribed to the religious leaders in Luke 11:42.

10. Forster, *Aspects of the Novel*, 103–18.

11. Abrams, *Glossary*, 185.

12. Ibid., 48.

13. Ibid., 49.

14. This phenomenon is best documented with regard to the Gospel of Matthew, where the specific designation sometimes changes inexplicably within a single episode (cf. 21:23, 45). See Sjef Van Tilborg, *The Jewish Leaders in Matthew* (Leiden: Brill, 1972), 171–72. Mark and Luke are more careful, but even here "the scribes" serves as an ambiguous reference found throughout both Gospels and in combinations with practically all other groups.

15. See, for example, Jack Dean Kingsbury, "The Developing Conflict Between Jesus and the Jewish Leaders in Matthew's Gospel: A Literary-Critical Study," *CBQ* 49 (1987): 57–73; Mark Allan Powell, "The Religious Leaders in Luke: A Literary-Critical Study," *JBL* 109 (1990): 103–20; Stephen H. Smith, "The Role of Jesus' Opponents in the Markan Drama," *NTS* 35 (1989): 161–82. On subgroups, cf. Elizabeth Struthers Malbon, "The Religious Leaders in the Gospel of Mark: A Literary Study of Markan Characterization," *JBL* 108 (1989): 259–81; John T. Carroll, "Luke's Portrayal of the Pharisees," *CBQ* 50 (1988): 604–21.

16. Although Luke does not specify religious leaders as the audience for the parable of Jesus in 18:10-14, the parable itself presents a religious leader as exemplary of people who exhibit the traits listed in 18:9.

17. For detailed analysis of such passages in Matthew, see Mark Allan Powell, "The Religious Leaders in Matthew: A Literary Critical Approach," (Ph. D. diss., Union Theological Seminary in Virginia, 1988), 177–82. On Mark, see Joanna Dewey, *Markan Public Debate: Literary Technique, Concentric Structure and Theology in Mark 2:1—3:6*, SBLDS 48 (Chico, Calif.: Scholars Press, 1980). In Luke the pattern is less consistent, but still discernible.

18. In Luke, their avoidance of direct criticism applies only to Jesus, not to his disciples (cf. 5:30; 6:2).

19. Gerhard Barth, "Matthew's Understanding of the Law," in Günther Bornkamm, Gerhard Barth, and H. J. Held, *Tradition and Interpretation in Matthew*, trans. P. Scott (Philadelphia: Westminster, 1963), 105–12.

20. This point, and the discussion on character traits in Mark that follows, is heavily indebted to Kingsbury, *Conflict in Mark: Jesus, Authorities, Disciples* (Minneapolis: Fortress Press, 1989), 14–21.

21. Meir Sternberg notes the literary importance of "the primary effect," by which information conveyed early in the narrative shapes the reader's perception most critically. See *Expositional Modes and Temporal Ordering in Fiction* (Baltimore: John Hopkins University Press, 1978), 102–04.

22. Kingsbury, *Matthew As Story*, 19.

23. The closest Jesus ever comes to calling them evil in Luke is to say that they are "full of wickedness" (11:39). Here, the point is not to describe their basic nature but to give the lie to their deceptively clean appearance. Furthermore, the wickedness is something of which they can be clean (11:40).

24. This assumes that 23:2-3 is to be taken ironically. As for 8:18-22, see Jack Dean Kingsbury, "The 'Eager' Scribe and the 'Reluctant' Disciple (Matt. 8:18-22)," *NTS* 34 (1988): 45–59.

25. Some do, of course, in the book of Acts—notably Saul (Paul). Luke also instills some hope for the religious leaders in his Gospel by bracketing their story with accounts of "exceptions." Zechariah and Joseph of Arimathea, the first and the last religious leaders in the story, are explicitly characterized as "righteous" (1:6; 23:50) and so serve as reminders that the portrayal of leaders elsewhere in the narrative need not be regarded as absolute.

26. Cf. Tannehill, *Narrative Unity*, vol. 1, 8–9.

27. Kingsbury, *Conflict in Mark*, 66–67.

Chapter 6: Settings

1. Cf. Rhoads and Michie, *Mark As Story*, 63.

2. Chatman, *Story and Discourse*, 138–41. Chatman rejects the validity of such criteria as biology, identity (possessing a name), and importance to the plot for making absolute distinctions. Elsewhere, Wesley Kort has concentrated on settings as elements that are "beyond the reach of human influence, modification, and control." See Kort, *Narrative Elements and Religious Meanings* (Philadelphia: Fortress Press, 1975), 20–21. This definition, however, applies only to what he calls "atmosphere," and does not serve, for instance, to distinguish a boat from the people who sail it. In my view, the boat can be called a setting if it does not espouse a particular point of view and the people can be called characters if they do.

3. Rhoads and Michie, *Mark As Story*, 63.

4. Chatman, *Story and Discourse*, 141.

5. Abrams, *Glossary*, 175.

6. Mieke Bal, *Narratology: Introduction to the Theology of Narrative* (Toronto: University of Toronto Press, 1985), 45–46, 94.

7. Literary critics do not agree on the appropriateness of such descriptions. See D. S. Bland, "Endangering The Reader's Neck: Background Description in the Novel," in Phillip Stevick, *The Theory of the Novel* (New York: Free Press, 1964), 313–31.

8. Bal, *Narratology*, 94.

9. Funk, *Poetics*, 141.

10. *The Jewish War* 5.212–14. David Ulansey, "The Heavenly Veil Torn: Cosmic Symbolism in the Gospel of Mark," unpublished paper presented at 1988 SBL annual meeting, Synoptic Gospels Section.

11. Typological references should not be simply equated with use of the adverbial genitive in Greek. The locative case is used in Mark 3:2, but context suggests the reference is primarily typological with regard to temporal setting.

12. In Matthew, for example, episodes are often introduced with the single word, *then*. In Mark, the preferred term is *immediately*.

13. The ironic link between these two women may be even greater if the "flow of blood" is understood as a reference to menstruation and "12 years of age" as a reference to the approximate onset of puberty. Cf. Herman C. Waetjen, *A Reordering of Power: A Socio-Political Reading of Mark's Gospel* (Minneapolis: Fortress Press, 1989), 122.

14. See Paul Ricoeur, *Time and Narrative*, 3 vols. (Chicago: University of Chicago Press, 1984, 1986, 1988). The concept of monumental time is developed primarily in the second and third volumes.

15. Rhoads, "Narrative Criticism," 413.

16. Rhoads and Michie, *Mark as Story*, 63–72, esp. 65–67.

17. Elizabeth Struthers Malbon, *Narrative Space and Mythic Meaning in Mark* (San Francisco: Harper & Row, 1986). Malbon utilizes Levi-Strauss's scheme of structural analysis.

18. See also Sean Freyne, *Galilee, Jesus, and the Gospels: Literary Approaches and Historical Investigations* (Philadelphia: Fortress Press, 1988), 63–68.

19. Rhoads and Michie, *Mark As Story*, 64–65.

20. Ibid., 64.

21. Dan Via, *The Ethics of Mark's Gospel in the Middle of Time* (Philadelphia: Fortress Press, 1985).

22. Genette, *Narrative Discourse*, 72.

23. There are no references in Mark, as there are in Luke-Acts, to events that take months (cf. Luke 1:56) or even years (Acts 11:26; 18:11). Even Mark 4:25 does not refer to time that passes within the narrated story.

24. Compare the story told by Luke, in which Jesus comes to proclaim the acceptable *year* of the Lord" (4:19).

25. The Greek expression in both Mark 1:35 and 16:2 is a combination of *lian* (very) with *proi* (early or in the morning). In 1:35 this apparently refers to a time just before sunrise, and in 16:2 to a time just following sunrise.

119

26. See Bruce Malina, *The New Testament World. Insights From Cultural Anthropology* (Atlanta: John Knox Press, 1981). Malina discusses the pivotal value assigned to honor and shame, the lack of individualism, the economic perception of limited good, the place of kinship and marriage, and the understanding of purity and impurity in first-century Mediterranean society.

27. Waetjen, *Reordering of Power*, 117–18.

28. On such movements, see Richard Horsley with John Hanson, *Bandits, Prophets, and Messiahs. Popular Movements at the Time of Jesus* (San Francisco: Harper & Row, 1985).

Chapter 7: Story as Scripture

1. Robert Karris, *Luke: Artist and Theologian. Luke's Passion Account As Literature.* TI (New York: Paulist Press, 1985).

2. William Farmer, "Source Criticism: Some Comments on the Present Situation," *USQR* 42 (1988): 49–57, esp. 53. Farmer's comments are in reference to literary studies that I would call composition criticism, but his point certainly applies to narrative criticism as well.

3. See, for example, Theodore Weeden, *Traditions in Conflict* (Philadelphia: Fortress Press, 1971).

4. See, for example, Ernest Best, *Disciples and Discipleship: Studies in the Gospel According to Mark* (Edinburgh: T & T Clark, 1986).

5. Colin E. Gunton, *Enlightenment and Alienation: An Essay Towards a Trinitarian Theology* (Grand Rapids, Mich.: Eerdmans, 1985), 111.

6. The phrase is roughly equivalent to what Luther meant by "the literal meaning" of Scripture. Luther did not mean to equate "literally true" with "historically accurate." For a summary of Frei's view, see Kathryn E. Tanner, "Theology and the Plain Sense," in Garret Green, *Scriptural Authority and Narrative Interpretation* (Philadelphia: Fortress Press, 1987), 59–78.

7. Narrative criticism deals with this problem in exactly the opposite manner than did Bultmann's program for demythologizing. Bultmann attempted to abstract moral or philosophical truth from texts by translating the mythological framework into categories of existentialist philosophy. Narrative criticism regards the meaning of texts as inseparable from the form in which it is expressed, and so embraces the story (myth and all) as a world to be entered and experienced. See Lynn Poland, *Literary Criticism and Biblical Hermeneutics*, AARAS 48 (Chico, Calif.: Scholars Press, 1985), 22–53.

8. See the discussion of the religious leaders in Matthew in chapter 5 of this book.

9. Alan Culpepper, "Story and History in the Gospels," *RevExp* 81 (1984): 467–77, esp. 473.

10. Tremper Longman, for instance, endorses modern literary study of the Bible while maintaining that the text is also referential and, in fact, "inerrant" in its historical representation. Sally McFague, on the other hand, favors literary approaches to the Bible because she regards the Bible as authoritative only in that it is a "literary classic that continues to speak to us." Cf. Longman, "Storytellers and Poets in the Bible. Can Literary Artifice Be True?" in H. Conn, *Inerrancy and Hermeneutic. A Tradition, A Challenge,*

A Debate (Grand Rapids, Mich.: Baker Book House, 1988), 137–49; McFague, *Speaking in Parables* (Philadelphia: Fortress Press, 1975); idem, *Metaphorical Theology: Models of God in Religious Language* (Philadelphia: Fortress Press, 1982).

11. Lonnie Kliever, *The Shattered Spectrum: A Survey of Contemporary Theology* (Atlanta: John Knox Press, 1981), 156.

12. Culpepper, "Story and History," 470.

13. Ibid., 474.

14. See Culpepper, *Anatomy of Fourth Gospel*, 8–11 and Longman, *Literary Approaches*, 47–58.

15. Karl Ludwig Schmidt, *Der Rahmen der Geschichte Jesu* (Darmstadt: Wissenschaftliche Buchgesellschaft, 1964; first published 1919).

16. Roland Mushat Frye, "A Literary Perspective for the Criticism of the Gospels," in D. G. Miller and D. Y. Hadidian, *Jesus and Man's Hope* (Pittsburg: Pittsburg Theological Seminary Press, 1971), 192–221, esp. 220 n. 42.

17. Stephen Moore, "Are the Gospels Unified Narratives?" in *SBL 1987 Seminar Papers*, (Atlanta, Ga.: Scholars Press, 1987), 443–58.

18. *Contra* Petersen ("Point of View in Mark's Narrative," 104) and Moore ("Are the Gospels Unified Narratives?" 452 n. 56).

19. Both Tannehill (*Narrative Unity*) and Dawsey (*Lukan Voice*) offer reasonable explanations for how a reader will interpret the apparent inconsistencies between Luke 1–2 and the rest of this Gospel (I prefer Tannehill). Moore ("Are the Gospels Unified Narratives?") reviews these proposals and finds both inadequate to establish the unity of Luke's work. The point, however, is to describe how a person who does read the narrative as a unity will make sense of the inconsistencies that are there.

20. Auerbach, *Mimesis*. See the discussion in chapter 1 of this book.

21. Frye, *The Great Code*, 46–47.

22. Christopher Tuckett, *Reading the New Testament. Methods of Interpretation* (Philadelphia: Fortress Press, 1987), 174–75.

23. Ibid., 175, 179–80.

24. Some literary critics have disparaged traditional approaches in their support of new disciplines. Such "rhetorical shock tactics" were also used, and later regretted, by early proponents of New Criticism in secular circles. See McKnight, *Bible and the Reader*, 3–4.

25. Poland, *Literary Criticism*, 4.

26. Iser, *The Implied Reader*. The term is not defined, but is used frequently (see references listed in the subject index).

27. Scholars usually assume that historical questions such as whether Mark's Gospel was written before or after the destruction of Jerusalem in A.D. 70 are irrelevant for narrative criticism, but this might not be the case. Wayne Booth cites a modern novel set during the early 1960s that achieves its sense of impending doom only if the reader knows that President Kennedy is going to be assassinated (*Rhetoric of Fiction*, 423). Similarly, proposals regarding the intended literary effect of Mark's Gospel might have to take into account the question of whether this narrative assumes its reader knows what will happen to Jerusalem.

28. The term *index* is helpful because it connotes an indirect or general indication of something without implying specificity or certainty. See Kingsbury, "Reflections on 'the Reader,'" 459.

29. Cf. Wolfgang Iser's thesis that texts do not really contain meaning, but rather produce effects on those who read them: "The text represents a potential effect to be realized in the reading process" (*Act of Reading*, ix). Similarly Bultmann preferred to say that the New Testament "becomes" the Word of God when appropriated in faith. See Poland, *Literary Criticism*, 32.

30. Poland, *Literary Criticism*, 20. On Luther as an interpreter of Scripture, see *Int* 37/3 (July, 1983).

31. Culpepper, "Story and History," 475.

32. Frei, *Eclipse of Biblical Narrative*.

33. See Krister Stendahl, "Biblical Theology, Contemporary," *IDB*, vol 1: 418–31 (Nashville: Abingdon Press, 1962).

34. The terminology derives from Thomas Kuhn's *The Structure of Scientific Revolutions*, 2d ed. (Chicago: University of Chicago Press, 1970).

35. Leander Keck, "Will the Historical-Critical Method Survive?" in Spencer, *Orientation by Disorientation*, 115–27.

36. Culpepper, "Story and History," 473. For this reason, the method is misused when employed in order to give theologians "breathing room" or to allow them to "duck awkward questions" about truth. See Green, "The Bible As . . .': Fictional Narrative and Scriptural Truth," in *Scriptural Authority and Narrative Interpretation* 79–96, esp. 80.

37. Stephen Moore notes that "story-centered critics have not as yet shown any inclination to mount a systematic investigation of the theologies of the Gospel and Acts" (*Literary Criticism*, 58). Could this be because they recognize the limits of their discipline?

38. Maurice Wiles suggests that, while such a reading of the Bible might technically be possible, we would have to regard the story thus produced a "a very bad one." See "Scriptural Authority and Theological Construction: The Limitations of Narrative Interpretation," in Green, *Scriptural Authority and Narrative Interpretation*, 42–58, esp. 48.

39. This analogy was suggested to me by Ron Hals.

For Further Reading

For an extensive, annotated bibliography, see Mark Allan Powell, *The Bible and Modern Literary Criticism: A Critical Assessment and Annotated Bibliography* (Westport, Conn.: Greenwood Press, 1991).

PART 1: SECULAR LITERARY THEORY

Abrams, Meyer Howard. *A Glossary of Literary Terms*. 4th ed. New York: Holt, Rhinehart and Winston, 1981.

Bal, Mieke. *Narratology: Introduction to the Theory of Narrative*. Trans. C. von Boheemen. Toronto: University of Toronto Press, 1985.

Booth, Wayne. *The Rhetoric of Fiction*. 2d ed. Chicago: University of Chicago Press, 1983.

Brooks, Peter. *Reading for the Plot: Design and Intention in Narrative*. New York: Alfred A. Knopf, 1984.

Chatman, Seymour. *Story and Discourse: Narrative Structure in Fiction and Film*. Ithaca, N.Y.: Cornell University Press, 1978.

Forster, Edward Morgan. *Aspects of the Novel*. New York: Harcourt, Brace, Jovanovich, 1927.

Fowler, Roger, ed. *Style and Structure in Literature. Essays in the New Stylistics*. Ithaca, N.Y.: Cornell University Press, 1975.

Genette, Gerard. *Narrative Discourse: An Essay in Method*. Trans. J. Lewin. Ithaca, N.Y.: Cornell University Press, 1980.

Harvey, W. J. *Character and the Novel*. Ithaca, N.Y.: Cornell University Press, 1965.

Iser, Wolfgang. *The Act of Reading: A Theory of Aesthetic Response*. Baltimore: Johns Hopkins University Press, 1978.

Iser, Wolfgang. *The Implied Reader: Patterns of Communication in Prose Fiction from Bunyan to Beckett*. Baltimore: Johns Hopkins University Press, 1974.

Kermode, Frank. *The Art of Telling. Essays on Fiction*. Cambridge: Harvard University Press, 1983.

Kermode, Frank. *The Sense of an Ending: Studies in the Theory of Fiction*. New York: Oxford University Press, 1967.

Kort, Wesley. *Narrative Elements and Religious Meanings*. Philadelphia: Fortress Press, 1975.

Lanser, Susan Sniader. *The Narrative Act: Point of View in Prose Fiction.* Princeton: Princeton University Press, 1981.

Leitch, Thomas. *What Stories Are: Narrative Theory and Interpretation.* University Park, Pa.: Pennsylvania State University Press, 1986.

Martin, Wallace. *Recent Theories of Narrative.* Ithaca, N.Y.: Cornell University Press, 1986.

Mitchell, W. J. T., ed. *On Narrative.* Chicago: University of Chicago Press, 1981.

Perrine, Laurence. *Story and Structure.* 4th ed. New York: Harcourt, Brace, Jovanovich, 1974.

Prince, Gerald. *A Grammar of Stories: An Introduction.* The Hague: Mouton Publishers, 1973.

Prince, Gerald. *Narratology: The Form and Functioning of Narrative.* Berlin: Mouton Publishers, 1982.

Rimmon-Kenan, Shlomith. *Narrative Fiction: Contemporary Poetics.* London: Methuen, 1983.

Scholes, Robert, ed. *Approaches to the Novel: Materials for a Poetics.* Rev. ed. San Francisco: Chandler Publishing Co., 1966.

Scholes, Robert, and Kellogg, Robert. *The Nature of Narrative.* New York: Oxford University Press, 1966.

Stanzel, Franz K. *A Theory of Narrative.* Trans. C. Goedsche. Cambridge: Cambridge University Press, 1984.

Stevick, Phillip, ed. *The Theory of the Novel.* New York: Free Press, 1964.

Uspensky, Boris. *A Poetics of Composition: The Structure of the Artistic Text and Typology of a Compositional Form.* Trans. V. Zavarin and S. Wittig. Berkeley and Los Angeles: University of California Press, 1973.

Wellek, Rene, and Warren, Austin. *Theory of Literature.* 3d ed. San Diego: Harcourt, Brace, Jovanovich, 1975.

PART 2: LITERARY CRITICISM AND BIBLICAL NARRATIVE

Alter, Robert. *The Art of Biblical Narrative.* New York: Basic Books, 1981.

Beardslee, William A. *Literary Criticism of the New Testament.* GBS. Philadelphia: Fortress Press, 1969.

Berlin, Adele. *Poetics and Interpretation of Biblical Narrative.* Sheffield: Almond Press, 1983.

Clines, D.; Gunn, D.; and Hauser, A., eds. *Art and Meaning. Rhetoric in Biblical Literature.* JSOTSS 19. Sheffield: JSOT Press, 1982.

Culpepper, R. Alan. *Anatomy of the Fourth Gospel: A Study in Literary Design.* Philadelphia: Fortress Press, 1983.

Frei, Hans W. *The Eclipse of Biblical Narrative. A Study in Eighteenth and Nineteenth Century Hermeneutics.* New Haven, Conn.: Yale University Press, 1974.

Frye, Northrop. *The Great Code: The Bible and Literature.* New York: Harcourt, Brace, Jovanovich, 1982.

Funk, Robert W. *The Poetics of Biblical Narrative.* Sonoma, Calif.: Polebridge Press, 1988.

124

Green, Garrett, ed. *Scriptural Authority and Narrative Interpretation*. Philadelphia: Fortress Press, 1987.

Jasper, David. *The New Testament and the Literary Imagination*. Atlantic Highlands, N.J.: Humanities Press, 1987.

Keegan, Terence. *Interpreting the Bible: A Popular Introduction to Biblical Hermeneutics*. New York: Paulist Press, 1985.

Kermode, Frank. *The Genesis of Secrecy: On the Interpretation of Narrative*. Cambridge: Harvard University Press, 1979.

Kingsbury, Jack Dean. *Conflict in Luke: Jesus, Authorities, Disciples*. Minneapolis: Fortress Press, 1991.

Kingsbury, Jack Dean. *Conflict in Mark: Jesus, Authorities, Disciples*. Minneapolis: Fortress Press, 1989.

Kingsbury, Jack Dean. *Matthew As Story*. 2d edition. Philadelphia: Fortress Press, 1988.

Kingsbury, Jack Dean. *The Christology of Mark's Gospel*. Philadelphia: Fortress Press, 1983.

Kort, Wesley. *Story, Text, and Scripture. Literary Interests in Biblical Narrative*. University Park, Pa.: Pennsylvania State University Press, 1988.

Longman, Tremper. *Literary Approaches to Biblical Interpretation*. Grand Rapids, Mich.: Zondervan, 1987.

McKnight, Edgar. *The Bible and the Reader. An Introduction to Literary Criticism*. Philadelphia: Fortress Press, 1985.

Moore, Stephen. *Literary Criticism and the Gospels: The Theoretical Challenge*. New Haven, Conn.: Yale University Press, 1989.

Petersen, Norman R. *Literary Criticism for New Testament Critics*. GBS. Philadelphia: Fortress Press, 1978.

Poland, Lynn. *Literary Criticism and Biblical Hermeneutics*. AARAS 48. Chico, Calif.: Scholar's Press, 1985.

Rhoads, David and Michie, Donald. *Mark As Story: An Introduction to the Narrative of a Gospel*. Philadelphia: Fortress Press, 1982.

Spencer, Richard, ed. *Orientation by Disorientation. Studies in Literary Criticism and Biblical Literary Criticism Presented in Honor of William A. Beardslee*. PTMS 35. Pittsburgh: Pickwick Press, 1980.

Sternberg, Meir. *The Poetics of Biblical Narrative: Ideological Literature and the Drama of Reading*. Bloomington, Ind.: Indiana University Press, 1985.

Talbert, Mary Ann. *Sowing the Gospel: Mark's World in Literary-Historical Perspective*. Minneapolis: Fortres Press, 1989.

Tannehill, Robert. *The Narrative Unity of Luke-Acts: A Literary Interpretation*. 2 vols. Philadelphia and Minneapolis: Fortress Press, 1986 and 1990.

529-6960